Stuck Culture

The Great Stagnation

By

Marcus Lears

Marcus Lears

"Society is held together by duct tape, and a lot of these fragile mechanisms are starting to break down."

— **Tim Dillon,** *Comedian*

Marcus Lears

Table of Contents

Introduction: *The Cultural Time Loop*

Have you ever felt a strange sense of déjà vu while scrolling through your social media feed? As if you've seen that movie before, heard that song countless times, or witnessed that fashion trend cycle back around? Congratulations! You're not losing your mind—you're just trapped in the endless rerun of modern culture, where creativity seems to have taken an extended vacation.

This book, "Stuck Culture: The Great Stagnation," explores the curious phenomenon of cultural stagnation that has gripped our society since the mid-2000s. We'll examine how technology, which promised to usher in a new era of innovation, has instead become a nostalgia-powered hamster wheel, keeping us busy while we go nowhere fast. From Hollywood's obsession with reboots to the music industry's apparent time machine stuck in the 80s, we're living in a world where "cutting-edge" often means "we've cut and pasted something from 20 years ago."

But why does this matter? Because culture is the heartbeat of society, driving progress and shaping our collective future. When culture stagnates, so does innovation, critical thinking, and our ability to tackle the challenges of tomorrow. And let's face it, do we really need another superhero origin story or a "groundbreaking" fashion trend that's just your grandpa's old sweater with a designer label?

As we journey through these pages, we'll confront uncomfortable truths about our consumption habits and the corporate interests that benefit from our cultural inertia. We'll ask tough questions: Why do we cling to the familiar like it's the last lifeboat on the Titanic? How can we break free from this loop without triggering a collective existential crisis? What would a truly innovative culture look like in the 21st century, and would we even recognize it if it didn't come with a heavy dose of nostalgia?

This isn't just an academic exercise—it's a call to action. By understanding the forces at play, we can start to imagine a way out of this creative cul-de-sac. Are you ready to challenge the status quo and rediscover the thrill of genuine cultural evolution? Or will you tweet about it and go back to binge-watching that show you've already seen a dozen times? Let's begin this journcy through the past, present, and possibly-not-so-original future of culture.

Chapter 1: The Great Freeze: Why Culture Stopped Changing

The cultural scene of the mid-20th century was like a vibrant explosion of creativity and innovation. Imagine the 1950s—a time of hope and renewal as the world slowly crawled out from the shadows of war. This was when youth culture began to shape its own identity, marking a pivotal moment that sparked a wave of artistic expression. From the electrifying beats of rock and roll to the striking colors of abstract art, it felt like creativity was finally stretching its wings after being held back for so long.

Rock and roll emerged as the heartbeat of a new generation, blending rhythm and blues, country, and gospel into something fresh and exciting. Icons like Chuck Berry and Elvis Presley didn't just produce music; they sparked a cultural shift that challenged the norms of society, pushing against the limits of a more conservative world. Teens, energized by the music, began to express their individuality and demand their place in a society that often overlooked them. The unimaginable happened: a generation wasn't just soaking up culture; they were actively shaping it. Music transformed from mere entertainment into a powerful force for change—serving as the anthem for civil rights and a shout for personal freedom.

Zoom ahead a decade or two, and the 1960s and 1970s brought a new wave of activism. This was the time when counterculture movements thrived. The Beatles didn't just change music; they redefined pop culture itself, pushing the boundaries of artistic expression. Their experimental sounds and psychedelic visuals mirrored the chaotic political landscape of the day. The Vietnam War, civil rights marches, and the push for gender equality set the stage for art that bravely tackled uncomfortable truths. Music festivals like Woodstock became more than just concerts; they were cultural milestones, celebrating ideals of peace, love, and community.

Fashion also became an important way for people to express themselves. Designers like André Courrèges and Yves Saint Laurent stepped away from the ordinary, embracing daring styles that reflected the excitement of the era. Miniskirts, bell-bottoms, and psychedelic patterns were more than just clothing; they were bold statements. People used fashion to show who they were and what they stood for. In this charged environment, creativity thrived as traditional forms were constantly challenged in favor of the new and experimental.

When the 1980s arrived, the cultural scene kept evolving at a thrilling pace. The rise of hip-hop, especially in urban areas like New York City, introduced not only a new genre but also a meaningful cultural movement. Hip-hop became a voice for the unheard, providing a space where stories of struggle and resilience could shine. Graffiti artists, breakdancers, and DJs created a vibrant underground culture that would eventually reach mainstream audiences. The launch of MTV changed how music was experienced, turning music videos into a powerful art form. It was a time when visuals and sounds merged to create a whole new way of enjoying art.

In the early 1990s, grunge, alternative rock, and the riot grrrl movement began to emerge. Bands like Nirvana and pioneering female punk rockers like Bikini Kill challenged the established norms, offering a raw, unrefined view of life that connected deeply with disillusioned youth. Their art wasn't polished, but it was genuine. It resonated with a generation wrestling with questions of identity and purpose amid the harsh realities of the world.

Yet, as the mid-2000s approached, a noticeable change began to take place. The incredible cultural revolution that had defined the previous decades started to stall. Creativity didn't disappear; instead, it felt like the environments that once nurtured innovation transformed into obstacles. The excitement of the 90s and the rebellious spirit of earlier movements seemed to fade, giving way to a sense of nostalgia for what had come before. The revolutionary energy that had driven culture forward began to diminish, setting the stage for a very different cultural landscape that was about to emerge.

The Threshold of Stagnation

The mid-2000s was a turning point for culture, a time when the creative energy that fueled earlier decades started to feel the weight of new limitations. In 2007, the launch of the iPhone signaled the start of a fresh chapter—not just in how we communicate but in the very way we connect with culture. This sleek device, with its simple design and user-friendly interface, became a beacon of our increasingly digital lives. It was more than just a phone; it was a gateway to a never-ending flow of information, entertainment, and social interaction. With just a few taps and swipes, people could access a symphony of sounds, a wealth of visual art, and a library of literature—all from the comfort of their palms.

However, this incredible access to culture also brought about a significant change in how we experienced it. The iPhone shifted our relationship with music, art, and media, placing a greater emphasis on speed rather than depth. Gone were the days when individuals would wander into record stores to discover new music or browse galleries to appreciate contemporary pieces. Now, any song or artwork was merely a click away, often leading to a more shallow engagement. The convenience of streaming music and videos allowed us to jump from one piece of content to the next, without ever truly soaking in any particular work. This hurried consumption fostered a surface-level relationship with culture, where the excitement of discovery was overshadowed by an overwhelming abundance of choices.

As the iPhone opened the door to this new way of consuming culture, social media platforms began to emerge, further reshaping our cultural landscape. Facebook, Twitter, and later Instagram changed not just how we interacted with each other but also how we interacted with cultural expressions. These platforms offered new ways to express ourselves, allowing anyone with an internet connection to share their thoughts, art, and experiences. Yet, this newfound freedom came with its own set of challenges. Instead of encouraging rich conversations among diverse viewpoints, social media often created echo chambers, reinforcing existing beliefs while blocking out contrasting ones. The algorithms behind these platforms prioritized engagement over meaningful interactions, causing users to gravitate toward familiar content instead of exploring new ideas.

In this new environment, louder voices frequently overshadowed the more thoughtful discussions that might have thrived elsewhere. A tweet could ignite a storm of conversation, but the depth of those discussions often fell flat. The speed at which we shared and reacted led to a culture that valued quickness over thoughtfulness. Instead of diving into a thought-provoking article or engaging with an intricate piece of art, we found ourselves mindlessly scrolling through endless updates and memes. The digital age introduced a new way of communicating, but it often leaned toward immediacy rather than reflection.

With social media taking center stage in our cultural dialogues, streaming services came along as another big player in this story of cultural stagnation. Platforms like Netflix, Spotify, and YouTube made vast libraries of content available at our fingertips. Audiences no longer had to wait for shows to air or albums to be released; they could binge-watch entire series or listen to an artist's complete work in one go. While this expansion of media access opened doors for many creators, it also birthed a concerning trend. The ease of finding familiar content often dampened the urge to seek out new and innovative works. People began to prefer the comfort of nostalgia, revisiting beloved shows and artists instead of daring to explore something new.

The binge-watching phenomenon illustrated this shift perfectly. Instead of savoring each episode of a show as it aired, viewers would consume entire seasons in a single weekend. This created a culture of instant gratification, where the excitement of waiting for the next episode was sacrificed for the quick pleasure of finishing a series. The once-thrilling joy of discovering a groundbreaking show or artist was replaced by a cycle of comfort and familiarity. This craving for the familiar overshadowed the opportunity for risk-taking and experimentation that had once characterized vibrant cultural movements.

In this atmosphere, originality often took a backseat to safety. Creators started to cling to tried-and-true formulas and recognizable genres to ensure their work would resonate with audiences who were more used to repetition than innovation. The cultural landscape that once celebrated bold expressions transformed into one that favored reboots, sequels, and remakes. In music, artists increasingly leaned on familiar sounds and nostalgic references to attract listeners, leading to a blending of musical styles and a hesitation to venture into new territories.

As these technological advancements converged, they unintentionally created a space of cultural stagnation. The structures that once encouraged creative risk-taking began to crumble, stifling the very forces that had driven culture forward in the past. What started as exciting breakthroughs in communication and entertainment slowly evolved into an environment where the thrill of the new faded, overshadowed by the comfort of what we already knew. The cultural landscape shifted as the fearless experimentation of days gone by gave way to an era of caution, where innovation retreated to the sidelines and nostalgia took the spotlight.

We had crossed the threshold of stagnation, and as we stepped into this new cultural paradigm, we were left to grapple with the impacts of an age that celebrated consumption over creation. The vibrant echoes of a revolutionary past faded into a quiet backdrop, leaving us to wonder what the future of culture might look like in a time defined by ease and familiarity. The challenge was clear: could we reignite the flames of creativity in a world where taking risks had become an afterthought?

Cultural Stagnation: The Hidden Forces at Play

In today's fast-paced world, filled with constant technological advancements and a seemingly endless range of entertainment options, the idea of cultural stagnation might seem surprising. How could culture come to a standstill when we are bombarded every day with new content? However, if we take a closer look, we uncover a deeper reality: cultural stagnation doesn't just come from a lack of fresh ideas or creative talent. Instead, it is deeply influenced by structural forces that shape our cultural world, particularly corporate interests and a strong sense of nostalgia.

Picture yourself walking through a modern art gallery, where every piece feels oddly familiar, like a reimagining of something you've seen before rather than something entirely new. This feeling isn't just in your head; it points to a troubling truth. Corporations are increasingly focused on profits over creativity as they try to dominate the cultural market. This focus leads to a uniformity in cultural products, where making money often takes precedence over taking risks with artistic exploration. The saying "If it ain't broke, don't fix it" has shifted to "If it's making money, make more of it." As a result, creators frequently find themselves nudged, or even pushed, into familiar molds that promise commercial success rather than encouraged to explore new ideas.

The influence of these corporate interests is also evident in how we, as consumers, interact with culture. Streaming services and social media algorithms are designed to keep us watching and engaged, but they often lead us down the same familiar paths. We get caught in loops of recommendations based on what we've watched before, constantly served up the same genres or styles we already know we like. The vast libraries of content that used to promise endless discovery now often keep us in the same well-trodden areas. In this way, the endless scroll becomes a paradox; the more options we have for engaging with different cultural expressions, the less likely we are to step outside our comfort zones.

On top of these corporate pressures is the heavy weight of nostalgia—a powerful force that significantly shapes how we consume culture. We often lean towards familiar stories, beloved characters, and iconic songs that spark fond memories. Nostalgia wraps us in the warmth of the past, but it can also hold us back from embracing new experiences. There's something undeniably captivating about looking back, a bittersweet reminder of simpler times that can make even the most ordinary moments feel special. But we need to ask ourselves: at what cost?

Take a moment to think about the trend of reboots and remakes in movies and TV shows. The popularity of these projects often relates not only to a creative team's desire for a quick win but also to our own longing to relive favorite stories. While there can be value in revisiting classics with modern twists, the overwhelming focus on nostalgia can drown out original narratives. This leads to a cultural landscape where true innovation struggles to emerge. The stories we once loved can become mere shadows of their former selves, recycled in ways that hardly capture the magic that made them great in the first place.

Yet, in the midst of this stagnation, there is a spark of hope. The creativity and talent needed for cultural evolution aren't gone; they're still here, waiting for the right moment to shine. Artists, writers, musicians, and creators are bursting with fresh ideas and new perspectives, yet these voices often get lost in the noise of corporate strategies and the pull of nostalgia. The real challenge is creating an environment where these talents can thrive—one where taking risks is encouraged and the unfamiliar is celebrated instead of feared.

Maybe the first step in reigniting this creative fire is for us, as consumers, to take a moment to reflect on our own habits. Are we unconsciously contributing to this stagnation by always reaching for the familiar? When we binge-watch the latest season of a beloved series or replay the soundtrack of our youth, are we unintentionally supporting a culture that prefers repetition over innovation? It's worth considering how our choices in entertainment shape the cultural landscape and what this means for the future of creativity.

Chapter 2: The Algorithm Trap: Culture Curated, Not Created

In today's world of digital content, there's a strange contradiction: the more we think we're in charge of our choices, the more we seem to be trapped by algorithms. Platforms like Spotify, Netflix, and YouTube have taken the lead in shaping our cultural experiences, deciding not only what we see, listen to, or read, but also influencing how we connect with culture itself. For many of us, this results in a never-ending stream of content that feels personalized and relevant. However, it often turns out to be repetitive and limited. We might think we're discovering exciting new things, but in reality, we often find ourselves stuck in a bubble of familiarity, buoyed by algorithms that are designed to keep us comfortable.

Think back to the last time you opened your favorite streaming service. You're greeted with a list of recommendations: "Since you liked X, you might enjoy Y." At first, this seems like a thoughtful nod to your preferences, recognizing the many factors that define what you like. But as you browse through the options, a troubling thought strikes you. How many of these picks are truly new or innovative? And how many are just more of the same, repackaged formulas that stick to what's predictable? This subtle form of consumption control has become our new normal.

Where did the vibrant mix of cultural experiences go that once made our media consumption so exciting? In the past, discovering an obscure indie film, an experimental band, or a thought-provoking documentary felt like a delightful surprise, something that happened by chance rather than through a carefully planned algorithm. Nowadays, the thrill of stumbling upon something unexpected has been replaced by a manufactured selection that keeps you glued to your screen, reducing your options to just a few safe choices. The result? A sameness in creativity that stifles originality and nurtures a culture stuck in a rut.

The impact of this trend reaches far beyond our personal viewing habits. When creators see that content fitting neatly into established patterns is successful, they often stick to those formulas, choosing what's proven to work over what could be daring. The temptation for viral success and algorithmic approval looms large, shaping decisions that should really be based on artistic vision. The boldness that once enriched our cultural landscape is being replaced by a cautious approach, where creators are driven to imitate the very trends that captured audiences, even if they feel stale.

Take the music industry, for example, where the streaming model has completely altered how songs are made. Thanks to platforms like Spotify, the idea of the "hit song" has taken over. Musicians now face pressure to create tracks that fit perfectly into playlists designed for specific moods or activities. This shift has pushed a formulaic style of songwriting, where songs are tailored for algorithms instead of genuine artistic expression. The focus on data-driven choices can stifle creativity, as artists produce catchy hooks and familiar beats aimed at securing a spot on playlists, often at the expense of their distinct voices.

This back-and-forth relationship between content consumers and creators forms a cycle that rewards what's already familiar. As audiences flock to algorithm-curated selections, it creates a feedback loop that reinforces itself. Creators see their safe bets succeed with streams and views, prompting platforms to promote even more of the same, which further limits the cultural landscape. When creators prioritize algorithmic success over their artistic vision, the whole ecosystem suffers, leading to less diversity in voices and experiences available to audiences.

We can't ignore the comfort that comes with algorithm-curated content. Familiarity breeds a sense of contentment, and there's a natural tendency for people to stick with what they know. That warm feeling of nostalgia, along with the easy access to beloved titles, can become a tempting trap. Why take a risk on something new when the safety of the familiar is just a click away? This isn't just a personal decision; it reflects a broader cultural trend with serious consequences.

The result is a shared experience that encourages stagnation rather than creativity. When we retreat to the familiar, we miss out on enriching experiences that challenge our views, expand our horizons, and spark our imaginations. The rich variety of cultural offerings that once thrived is pushed into the background, as the polished allure of algorithm-driven suggestions takes center stage. Our cultural fabric begins to fray as unique voices get drowned out by a chorus of repeating ideas and well-worn tropes.

A crucial moment arises when we consider what this control over consumption means for us. The key question becomes: how can we break free from the algorithmic chains that limit our cultural experiences? It starts with understanding our role as consumers. There's real power in the choices we make, and we can influence the kinds of content that get created and celebrated. If we actively seek out fresh perspectives, unique talents, and bold projects, we send a clear message to creators and platforms: we want diversity, we value innovation, and we're ready to step out of our comfort zones.

On a personal level, this could mean shaking up your cultural habits. Rather than just going with algorithm-driven suggestions, explore new genres, discover independent creators, or dive into the works of artists who have different backgrounds or experiences than you. Challenging your own preferences can lead to surprising joys and widen your understanding of the world. It's a small change, but it's a powerful way for consumers to reclaim their cultural experiences from the grip of algorithms.

Creators also play a crucial role in changing this landscape. By resisting the urge to create "safe" content, they can push the boundaries of what's possible. Artists shouldn't shy away from experimentation, collaboration, and taking risks; doing so can open doors to new stories and groundbreaking ideas that defy conventional categories. Choosing innovation over predictability can lead to the creation of works that resonate deeply with audiences, lighting a spark of inspiration that transcends algorithmic limits.

Together, consumers and creators can carve out a new path that prioritizes creativity and diversity over conformity and predictability. It's a cultural revival waiting to happen, but it requires a shared shift in mindset. The barriers that algorithms have built around our cultural experiences can be dismantled, piece by piece, as we engage with the arts, challenge our preferences, and seek out the unknown.

In this era of consumption control, let's remember the power of curiosity. Simply seeking, questioning, and exploring can lead us to cultural gems that lie just beyond our algorithm-driven feeds. A world full of untold stories, diverse voices, and innovative ideas awaits those who dare to look beyond the screen and truly connect with culture in all its forms.

Reclaiming our cultural landscape means embracing the messy, unpredictable nature of artistic expression. It's about fostering a conversation where creativity can thrive, free from the limits of commercial interests or algorithmic biases. The journey may seem challenging, but it's in this uncertainty that the seeds of innovation take root. By making intentional choices to diversify our consumption habits, encouraging boldness in creators, and nurturing an environment that celebrates originality, we can break free from the algorithm trap that has held us back.

Let's aim for a cultural ecosystem that champions risk-taking, exploration, and the limitless potential of human creativity. The algorithms may have shaped our past consumption habits, but they don't have to dictate our future experiences. The power is in our hands, and the time to use it wisely has arrived.

Engagement Feedback Loop

The digital age has changed not only how we enjoy content but also how creators go about their work. In a world where engagement metrics rule, the tricky balance between creativity and the approval of algorithms reveals an interesting contradiction. The engagement feedback loop—a cycle where creators produce content based on audience reactions—has transformed the way culture is made.

At the core of this loop are key performance indicators (KPIs), the metrics that determine what success looks like on platforms like YouTube, Instagram, and TikTok. From views to likes, shares, and completion rates, these numbers are more than just figures; they can make or break a creator's career. In a system that values measurable results over artistic quality, creativity risks becoming a byproduct of data instead of genuine inspiration.

Metrics, which used to help us understand what audiences liked, have turned into a roadmap for making content. For example, when a video goes viral or a song hits the top of the charts, other creators pay attention. The metrics behind that success become the guidelines for what they create next. A creator might find themselves mimicking trending styles, using flashy thumbnails, or copying popular music genres—all in the name of getting more engagement. This leads to a culture that favors what's familiar instead of what's groundbreaking.

Think about the busy world of social media influencers. The most popular creators tend to follow a similar recipe for success: catchy hooks, relatable content, and a polished look. These elements are fine-tuned to connect with audiences, like a well-oiled machine producing what's known to work. Yet, in this chase for likes and shares, the individual voices of creators often get lost in a flood of sameness. While the engagement feedback loop provides instant approval, it can unintentionally stifle the very innovation that brings cultural vibrancy.

The impact of these metrics goes beyond just individual creators; it affects the broader fabric of cultural production. The desire for predictability leads to the rise of formulaic content, whether in TV shows or movies. Take reality TV, for instance, where the same themes and storylines are recycled over and over. Shows featuring housewives, survivalists, or talent competitions have become so predictable they might as well write themselves. This move toward the tried-and-true isn't just a coincidence; it's a strategic choice to keep viewers coming back. After all, why take a chance on a new idea when a proven formula guarantees a steady flow of views?

The film industry reflects this trend as well. In recent years, we've seen a flood of sequels, reboots, and franchises. Studios often see established titles as safer investments, pushing original stories to the back burner. This means audiences are bombarded with familiar characters and plots, leaving little room for fresh storytelling. The feedback loop feeds itself: studios look to past successes for inspiration, while creators feel the pressure to stick to what's already been proven to work.

Creativity, which once thrived on taking risks and experimenting, often takes a backseat now. The pressure to create content that gets immediate engagement can make creators doubt their artistic instincts. Instead of pushing boundaries and exploring new ideas, they may end up second-guessing their choices, opting for what's known to work instead of what's truly innovative. The constant pursuit of likes and shares creates a mental strain, leaving many creators feeling obligated to follow the trends dictated by the metrics they track so closely.

This issue doesn't only affect creators; it also has broader implications for cultural diversity. As the engagement feedback loop promotes predictable content, audiences get used to receiving the same stories, styles, and voices. This lack of variety can stifle important social conversations and slow the evolution of cultural identity. When only a narrow range of experiences and perspectives gets highlighted, a wealth of creative potential goes unnoticed, uncelebrated, and unheard.

To illustrate the psychological pressures creators face, consider the words of a filmmaker who reminisced about the carefree spirit of early cinema. "Back in the day, filmmakers took risks," they said. "They didn't worry about how many likes their trailer would get before launching the full film. Now, there's this constant anxiety about whether people will connect with what I want to say or if I should just stick to what's already popular." This feeling resonates with many artists who struggle with the clash between their personal expression and the demands of an algorithm-driven world.

Musicians, too, find themselves caught in a similar bind. An established indie band might feel pressured to write catchy hooks and radio-friendly tracks to land a spot on popular playlists, leaving behind the raw, experimental sound that initially defined their music. The idea of "selling out" has shifted; it's no longer just about making money but about conforming to the metrics that drive visibility. A successful artist once shared, "You start to question your own voice. Is it worth chasing what feels right for you if it means risking everything for a few likes?"

As creators navigate this challenging landscape, the sense of community that once thrived has been overshadowed by competition. Instead of collaborating and pushing each other toward new ideas, creators often find themselves caught in a race for attention—one that can lead to burnout and disappointment. The engagement feedback loop, which should promote creativity, can ironically become a source of imposter syndrome and self-doubt.

Yet, within this cycle lies a chance for positive change. The same metrics that limit creativity can also spark conversations about the importance of innovation. By recognizing the pressures imposed by the engagement feedback loop, creators can begin to reclaim their artistic integrity, intentionally choosing to embrace experimentation over conformity. It takes bravery to challenge the norm, but when creators come together, they can inspire one another to break free from predictable patterns.

The evolution of cultural production calls for a collective awakening. Audiences need to realize their role in this ecosystem too. Instead of just mindlessly scrolling through algorithm-driven feeds, they can actively seek out diverse voices and unique viewpoints. By supporting creators who take risks and challenge the status quo, consumers can help reshape the narratives that dominate cultural conversations. A culture that celebrates originality instead of simply following trends can emerge from this partnership.

In an era defined by the engagement feedback loop and algorithmic control, the challenges tied to creativity may seem intimidating. But the potential for groundbreaking work is just beneath the surface. When both creators and audiences commit to breaking the cycle of predictability, they can cultivate an environment brimming with possibilities. Cultural production thrives on the unexpected, the unconventional, and the bold—qualities that algorithms often struggle to capture.

Ultimately, the engagement feedback loop tells two stories. On one side, it highlights the pressures creators face in a metrics-driven world. On the other, it underscores the potential for transformative change when artists and audiences choose to reject the comfort of the familiar. By nurturing a culture that values innovation and diversity, we can reclaim the vibrant, dynamic landscape that reflects the richness of our shared human experience.

As we navigate this complex terrain, it's important to remember that creativity is not just a restricted exercise in metrics. It's an adventure, one that flourishes through exploration, curiosity, and risk-taking. With every step we take toward embracing the unpredictable, we stand at the brink of a cultural revival—a resurgence that can reshape our collective narrative and rekindle the spirit of innovation lost in the engagement feedback loop. The time for this revival is now, and it invites us all to join in the journey toward a richer, more diverse cultural landscape.

Psychological Comfort

In a world buzzing with endless choices, the algorithms that shape our digital experiences have become experts at creating psychological comfort. They tap into emotions that run deep, especially the warm glow of nostalgia, to build an environment where familiarity feels safe. This isn't just a byproduct of technology; it's a carefully crafted strategy that plays on our natural desire to find solace in what we know, especially during unsettling times.

Nostalgia—the mix of happiness and longing for days gone by—can be both comforting and a bit stifling, depending on how it's used. Picture yourself scrolling through a streaming service, greeted by a list of shows and movies that remind you of your childhood or special moments from your past. Maybe it's a classic sitcom that brings back memories of cozy weekends with family or a beloved movie that takes you back to simpler times. Each time you click on one of these familiar titles, it wraps you in a comforting embrace and lets you escape from the stresses of today.

Studies show that when the world feels chaotic—like during financial downturns, political strife, or global pandemics—people often turn to nostalgic content for comfort. For instance, in 2020, streaming platforms saw a huge spike in viewership for shows and movies from earlier times. This trend highlights how, in stressful moments, we often find refuge in what feels familiar rather than facing the current challenges or exploring new options. Algorithms, skilled at understanding what users like, quickly adjust to this need by promoting content that soothes and reassures us. Nostalgia becomes more than just a fleeting feeling; it turns into a smart tool that keeps us engaged.

Risk aversion also plays a big role in this entire scene. As humans, we are naturally inclined to prefer what we know—the comfort of familiar over the uncertainty of the new. This concept, known as the familiarity principle, suggests that we tend to like things simply because they are familiar to us. So, when faced with a sea of options, we often gravitate toward the titles we recognize, even if there are other exciting or innovative choices out there.

Streaming platforms show this risk-averse behavior perfectly. When you open the app, you'll likely see a list labeled "Recommended for You," featuring shows or movies you've already watched or enjoyed. The algorithms are set up to highlight this familiar content because they don't want to risk losing your attention. Why take a chance on a quirky indie film or a foreign-language series when you can stick with what you know will make you feel good? This algorithmic curation mirrors our strong desire for comfort, reinforcing habits that favor the familiar while sidelining opportunities for exploration or growth.

The impact of this preference for comfort reaches far beyond individual choices; it sends ripples through our culture. As audiences increasingly lean towards comforting content, creative industries adapt, often choosing familiarity over new ideas. The result? A cultural landscape that risks becoming stagnant, where innovation takes a back seat to the desire to recreate past hits. The rise of remakes, reboots, and sequels in movies and TV is a clear sign of how audience preferences for the known shape what gets made. Instead of taking bold storytelling risks, studios often play it safe by revamping familiar tales with well-known characters, knowing they'll attract a guaranteed audience that won't stray far from what they love.

Yet, this trend can have serious long-term effects on creativity and cultural growth. When comfort becomes the main reason we consume content, the chances for artistic innovation start to fade. Creators may find themselves stuck in a cycle where the chase for familiarity limits their ability to experiment and explore new ideas, genres, or formats. The creative process shines when it embraces risk and pushes boundaries, but instead, it gets boxed in by the expectation to deliver what's safe and recognizable. The rich and colorful variety of cultural expression, once filled with diverse and unexpected stories, risks becoming a dull echo of what's already been done.

As society leans more into comfort-seeking behavior, the effects reach deep into our cultural identity. The cultural scene starts to blend together, as unique voices and perspectives struggle to be heard amid the flood of predictable content. When algorithms favor comfort over challenge, they unintentionally drown out lesser-known artists who dare to innovate or present fresh narratives. The fear of being overlooked can discourage creators, who might choose safer paths that fit audience expectations, further stifling innovation and cultural growth.

However, breaking away from the grip of algorithms isn't impossible. There are ways to expand our consumption, urging both creators and viewers to step outside the cozy confines of psychological comfort. For audiences, this means actively seeking out unfamiliar content. Rather than scrolling mindlessly through recommendations based on what you've watched before, take a step to explore genres or themes that might challenge your views. Streaming platforms can help with this by offering curated lists of innovative or lesser-known works, encouraging users to take a leap into something new.

At the same time, creators can resist the pressure to conform to algorithmic trends by focusing on authenticity instead of just chasing audience approval. They can embrace the discomfort that comes with taking risks and challenge themselves to move beyond familiar narratives. By fostering a spirit of experimentation, artists can spark curiosity in audiences, encouraging them to engage with content that's original and thought-provoking, reigniting a collective interest in the unfamiliar.

Some might argue that this cultural landscape, shaped by algorithmic influence and risk aversion, actually creates a unique chance for a cultural renaissance. Just as previous movements in art and literature have sprung from times of upheaval, now is a moment that calls for renewed dedication to creativity and innovation. By building an environment that values exploration and variety, both audiences and creators can work together to create a vibrant cultural scene that celebrates originality.

As we strive for a more dynamic cultural experience, it's crucial to remember that while nostalgia brings comfort, it shouldn't dictate our cultural choices. We can cherish our treasured memories while also welcoming the new and unfamiliar. The challenge lies in finding a balance between our natural desire for psychological comfort and the need for cultural diversity. By stepping outside our comfort zones, we open ourselves up to new experiences, stories, and perspectives that can enrich our shared imagination.

In the end, the psychological aspects of algorithm-driven consumption have a powerful impact on our experiences, shaping what we like and how we behave in significant ways. While algorithms may cater to our craving for comfort and familiarity, real transformative change lies in our hands. By intentionally diversifying what we watch and supporting creators willing to take risks, we can go beyond the limitations set by algorithms and create a cultural landscape that truly reflects the richness of our human experiences.

In this exciting new era of cultural consumption, the path toward innovation and creativity calls for both individual and collective effort. It invites us to embrace discomfort, question the status quo, and connect with a variety of voices and stories. As we navigate the complex links between technology, nostalgia, and our fear of the new, we find ourselves at a crucial point—a chance to redefine our relationship with culture and spark a wave of creativity that will resonate through generations. The algorithms may point the way, but it's our choices that will ultimately shape the narratives we tell and the culture we nurture.

Marcus Lears

Chapter 3: Hollywood on Repeat: Sequels, Remakes, and the Death of Risk

Hollywood has always danced to the unpredictable rhythm of the box office, where fortunes can swing wildly and determine the fate of not just individual films, but entire studios. The stakes are sky-high, and the pressure to turn a profit can feel overwhelming. Nowadays, when making a movie can cost hundreds of millions of dollars, it's no surprise that studio executives and investors lean towards projects that already have a fan base. This tendency has led to a world filled with sequels, remakes, and spin-offs that not only dominate our theater screens but also shape the conversations we have about movies.

There's something comforting about these familiar titles. They come with dedicated fans, well-known characters, and a sense of nostalgia that connects us to our past. The logic is straightforward: stick with what has worked before and watch the profits roll in. This approach makes sense in a cautious industry that is more wary of taking risks than ever. Why take a chance on a brand-new story when you can rely on the tried-and-true formula of a blockbuster that audiences already love?

Take a look at the recent blockbuster landscape. Franchises like "Marvel," "Star Wars," and "Jurassic Park" have turned into pop culture giants, producing numerous films, tons of merchandise, and a wide range of spin-off content. Each new installment is carefully crafted to meet fan expectations, driving box office success. This cycle has created a pressure cooker effect where studios feel they must keep these franchises alive, churning out more content to maximize their popularity.

The financial math that drives Hollywood also reflects a shift in the audience's make-up. A growing share of revenue is coming from international markets, each with its own tastes and preferences. This change pushes studios to favor stories that are universally appealing and reliant on established intellectual property (IP), rather than more intricate narratives that might resonate domestically but struggle to attract attention overseas.

In this environment, the original screenplay feels like a fading memory. The industry's focus on familiar tales mirrors a larger cultural shift—one that leans heavily towards caution and is shaped by what sells. In the past, a newcomer with a brilliant idea might find a platform for their story, but today, Hollywood seems to favor the safer route.

This cautious attitude isn't just a reaction to market conditions; it's become a core part of the industry's strategy. Executives are very aware of what their investors expect. They aren't just responsible for delivering enjoyable films; they also have to make sure those films make money. The result? A trend towards sequels and remakes that promise solid returns. While these films may not break new ground or push boundaries, they are viewed as safe bets, and that's the heart of the issue.

The rise of streaming services has also changed how audiences consume content. Now, people can binge-watch entire series and revisit their favorite films with just a click. This new way of watching favors content that's easily recognizable and straightforward. Audiences are drawn to these familiar titles, creating a cycle that encourages studios to keep making more sequels and remakes. It's ironic; even though technology has made it easier to access a wide variety of stories, it has also narrowed the range of tales that are actually told.

Now, consider the trend of reboots. These films often get criticized for being unoriginal, yet they continue to be produced at an astounding rate. The reasoning behind this is simple: audiences are more likely to go for something they already know rather than take a chance on something fresh and untested. This creates a loop; as studios embrace this model, audiences come to expect it, which makes it even tougher for new ideas to break through.

Let's not overlook the talented people behind these films. Screenwriters and directors who once yearned to share unique stories now face an uphill battle. The pressure to stick to what's safe can stifle creativity and limit chances for fresh voices to rise. When the industry places such a high value on the financially secure, the likelihood of seeing groundbreaking tales diminish. True creativity thrives on taking chances; it flourishes when artists are encouraged to explore new horizons.

The economic incentives that keep Hollywood stuck in this repetitive cycle are deeply connected to what audiences expect and the changes in technology. This creates a culture where originality often takes a backseat to profit. In the quest for safe returns, the industry finds itself caught in a loop, recycling past successes while ignoring the innovative potential that could be just around the corner. This ongoing cycle raises important questions about the future of storytelling in film and whether the creative spirit that once characterized Hollywood can survive in an environment so focused on financial gain.

As the industry navigates these waters, it's crucial to understand the wider impact of this trend. A media landscape dominated by repetition changes the very nature of storytelling and influences what we talk about as a society. The stories we choose to tell—or often retell—reflect our values and priorities. If we continue down this path of playing it safe and relying on familiar stories, what does that mean for the future of creativity in the arts?

The movie industry, like any other, must find a way to balance making money with nurturing creativity. While the financial reasons behind Hollywood's obsession with sequels and remakes are clear, the pressing question remains: at what price? The potential for a rich and diverse storytelling experience is hanging in the balance, waiting for an opportunity to embrace risk again. The challenge lies in breaking free from the chains of guaranteed profits and daring to explore new narratives that reflect our ever-changing world, instead of retreating into the comfort of the past.

The future of Hollywood may very well depend on its ability to redefine its relationship with risk. The industry needs to confront tough questions about what it truly means to be creative. Do we want to be providers of comfort and familiarity, or do we aspire to be trailblazers who challenge the norms? The answer, though complex, could shape the future of storytelling for years to come. In a world that is constantly changing, the demand for fresh and engaging stories is stronger than ever. It's up to the industry to rise to that challenge, to take bold leaps, and to embrace the unknown once more. The cinematic world needs voices that inspire, challenge, and spark our imaginations—voices that can only emerge when the tight grip of risk aversion is finally loosened.

Global Market Influence: The International Audience and Its Effects on Creativity

There was a time when Hollywood scriptwriters and directors could focus on creating stories just for American audiences. They had the freedom to explore the unique quirks of American culture and dive into the richness of the English language, all without worrying about how their work would fit into other languages or customs. But as the global marketplace has changed, so has the way stories are told in movies. Today, international audiences play a huge role in shaping how studios think about everything from character development to plotlines. This shift isn't just about convenience; it shows a significant change in the film industry's priorities, often putting profits ahead of creativity.

The movie industry's financial stakes have risen sharply, especially with the booming international box office revenues, particularly in countries like China. Foreign films, once considered niche, are now big players at the box office. The draw of these new markets is so strong that Hollywood is willing to go out of its way to appeal to them. Recent statistics show that around 35% of global box office revenue now comes from outside the United States.

This change has led studios to focus more on universal themes and broader appeal, sometimes sacrificing the storytelling details that could captivate local audiences. The result? Stories that can feel watered down, overly simplified, or scrubbed clean to avoid offending cultural sensibilities.

Hollywood's interaction with international markets raises important questions about artistic integrity and what storytelling truly means. Filmmakers now face the tough task of creating narratives that resonate with a wide range of cultures, which often involves navigating a maze of cultural sensitivities. Questions about how a film will be received in places with different cultural norms or political climates can lead to compromises in creativity. For instance, the animated movie "Kung Fu Panda" was praised for its respectful representation of Chinese martial arts, yet it faced criticism over how it depicted Asian culture. In a time when discussions around sensitivity training and cultural appropriation are everywhere, balancing respect for a culture with the need to succeed in the global market can feel like a tightrope walk.

Censoring and editing films for international audiences is another practice that serves as a double-edged sword. Take "Deadpool," for example, which was heavily edited for its release in China. The filmmakers had to cut out scenes that were deemed inappropriate, resulting in a version that, while still entertaining, was quite different from the original. Such alterations can lead to a film that feels less authentic—a mere shadow of what it could have been. While the motivation behind these changes is clear—studios want to maximize profits—the cost can be high. The original story's nuances may be lost, leaving viewers with a product that lacks its true spirit.

The focus on global markets also raises concerns about diversity and representation. Studios might hesitate to feature complex characters or bold narratives that could alienate specific audiences. With the pressure to appeal to a wide range of viewers, filmmakers might choose to stick with familiar archetypes and storylines that have proven to be commercially safe. This cautious approach often results in movies that follow a formula, missing the depth and originality that audiences genuinely want.

Conversations with industry insiders highlight the struggle filmmakers face between their artistic dreams and the financial pressures from big studios. Many express frustration over needing to compromise their vision, feeling stifled by an industry that prioritizes profits over creative exploration. The push for global appeal can lead to a standardization of films, where unique stories from diverse voices struggle to be heard amidst a sea of established franchises and safe choices.

To truly grasp how international factors have changed narrative choices, it helps to look at the different styles of films made for domestic audiences versus those crafted with a global view. Domestic films often allow for deeper storytelling that engages with specific social issues and reflects the complexities of American life. Movies like "Moonlight," which delves into race, sexuality, and identity, are prime examples of this trend. These films are willing to take risks, challenging norms and exploring themes that resonate with particular audiences.

In contrast, films created for global audiences typically stick to broad, easily understandable narratives that steer clear of controversial subjects. The "Transformers" franchise, for example, has been designed to prioritize action and spectacle over depth, delivering thrilling visuals and explosions that anyone can enjoy, regardless of their cultural background. While such films can do well at the box office, they often lack the emotional richness that characterizes more intimate storytelling. This trend towards spectacle highlights a significant difference between films that prioritize artistic expression and those that are made primarily for mass appeal.

As the lines blur between domestic and international markets, Hollywood finds itself at a crossroads. The understandable desire for profit conflicts with the need for creativity and innovation. The industry now has to find its way through the complexities of a global audience while still respecting the artistic impulses that inspire filmmakers. The challenge is to strike a balance between commercial interests and authentic storytelling, a task that's becoming more intricate in an industry that often favors the familiar over the groundbreaking.

When talking with filmmakers, a common feeling is one of frustration and disillusionment. Many believe that the demand for global appeal limits their ability to share personal stories that reflect their unique experiences and cultural backgrounds. This results in narratives that lean towards a more universal approach, losing out on the rich diversity of tales that could otherwise be told. The issue isn't just about missing new stories; it also raises serious concerns about what these choices mean for our culture as a whole. The stories we share shape how we understand the world, and narrowing these stories to what's commercially safe can have lasting impacts.

The ongoing trend of prioritizing global markets brings up critical questions about the future of creativity in Hollywood. As the industry struggles to stay profitable in a competitive landscape, the possibility for genuine storytelling hangs in the balance. Will filmmakers manage to reclaim their creative visions, or will they remain trapped by market demands? Unique storytellers deserve a place in the cinematic world, but they often get overshadowed by the lure of financial security.

It's vital for industry leaders to see the importance of taking risks in storytelling. Embracing a variety of narratives not only enriches the movie-watching experience but also expands the broader cultural conversation. The pressure to conform to global market trends shouldn't come at the expense of originality and authenticity. As audiences worldwide seek fresh stories and perspectives, Hollywood has a chance to rethink how it operates. By creating space for experimentation and innovation, studios can cultivate an environment where creativity thrives and diverse voices are amplified.

Ultimately, the real challenge is in redefining what it means to succeed in Hollywood. Is success simply measured by box office sales, or does it also include the impact that stories have on culture and society? As the industry evolves, it must address the complicated relationship between art and commerce, finding a way to achieve both profitability and genuine expression. The potential for rich storytelling is immense, waiting to be uncovered by filmmakers willing to break free from convention and embrace the diverse human experience.

Hollywood is at a crucial moment, one that could reshape its legacy for future generations. As the global audience grows in influence, the industry must find a way to meet their needs while staying true to the creative spirit that has always fueled storytelling. By valuing diverse narratives and allowing creativity to flourish, Hollywood can carve out a new path—one that mirrors the complexities of our world and celebrates the richness of human experiences. The challenge is significant, but the rewards of authenticity and innovation are undeniably worth the effort. The future of cinema hinges not just on which stories we decide to tell, but on how boldly we choose to share them.

Technological Irony: The Tools of Innovation Serving the Status Quo

The journey of filmmaking has been nothing short of extraordinary, echoing the larger story of how technology has advanced over the years. From the era of silent films with live music to the stunning practical effects in iconic movies like "Star Wars," and now to the dazzling CGI we see today, each technological leap has opened up new possibilities for storytelling. However, amidst this whirlwind of change, there's a troubling irony: the very tools meant to push creative boundaries often end up reinforcing the same old stories, decorating familiar narratives instead of exploring new ones.

In Hollywood's golden age, filmmakers leaned heavily on practical effects that showcased their inventiveness and hard work. The use of models, animatronics, and matte paintings were not just feats of technical skill; they were artistic achievements that allowed stories to truly thrive. For example, "The Wizard of Oz" masterfully blended these practical tricks with genuine human emotions, creating an unforgettable classic. The craftsmanship involved was tangible, and the magic of these films lay as much in the artistry as in the technology itself.

As the industry shifted into the realm of CGI, the beautiful artistry of practical effects took a step back. Suddenly, filmmakers had a digital toolbox that let them create entire worlds and characters that went beyond what was physically possible. The chance to bring dragons, alien planets, and fantastical beings to life with just a few clicks was revolutionary. However, over the years, this leap in technology hasn't always led to daring new stories. Instead, many filmmakers have chosen to use CGI to enhance and repackage well-known tales rather than crafting fresh narratives that truly engage the audience's imagination.

Today, remakes and sequels dominate the cinema landscape. The boom in franchises has created a mindset where studios seem to think revisiting familiar plots is the safest route. Films continually hit theaters, often packed with impressive new effects—be it CGI battles or stunning animated sequences—yet the stories themselves often stick to the same tired tropes. Recent reboots, like Disney's live-action versions of animated classics, illustrate this trend perfectly. Movies such as "The Lion King" and "Aladdin" offer breathtaking visuals but lean heavily on nostalgia instead of pushing the boundaries of storytelling. Instead of expanding the narrative world, they simply repackage familiar tales with cutting-edge technology.

This dependence on technology as a safety net in storytelling invites a deeper discussion about "franchise fatigue." Audiences are starting to notice the repetitive nature of big-budget films that prioritize style over substance. Sequels and spin-offs crowd the box office, filling theaters with recognizable characters and plotlines. Even when studios pour money into CGI, the emotional depth often feels shallow, overshadowed by recycled plots. The stunning visuals can serve as a mask, hiding uninspiring stories underneath. This gap between what technology can do and how it enhances storytelling raises important questions about creativity in Hollywood. Is the industry simply dressing up old favorites, or has it become too comfortable in its pursuit of profit?

Believing that technology alone can drive creativity is a risky misconception. While advancements in visual effects can certainly make a film look amazing, they need to be paired with a strong artistic vision to create meaningful stories. Without that guiding vision, technology can become a shiny distraction instead of a helpful tool for innovation. Filmmakers today are at a crossroads, caught between the lure of the latest tech and the need for deeper storytelling. Conversations with directors, visual effects supervisors, and writers reveal a common understanding of this struggle. Many express a wish to use technology to explore new stories, but they often feel limited by industry standards and the trend of playing it safe.

For instance, one emerging director shared his thoughts on how CGI should be used to connect with modern audiences: "We have all this incredible technology, but it feels like we're afraid to use it outside of established franchises," he expresses. "It's like we've forgotten how to dream. We have the tools to create new worlds, but instead, we keep circling back to the same ones." This sentiment is echoed by seasoned visual effects artists who have dedicated their careers to pushing creative boundaries. They see the potential for innovation within their craft, yet they feel pressured by the industry's expectations to stick to proven formulas. These voices reflect a broader frustration, hinting at a cultural stagnation in Hollywood that risks stifling creativity.

The main challenge now is figuring out how to use technology effectively without letting it dictate the story. Filmmakers need to be brave, using their creative instincts to shape their narratives. New technologies should be used to enhance unique stories, not just to dress up old ideas. Exciting developments like virtual reality and interactive storytelling have the potential to change the way stories are told, but they require a willingness to step outside the usual narrative structures.

Look at the rise of immersive storytelling experiences available through platforms like Oculus and other VR technologies. These innovations invite audiences to dive into narratives like never before, allowing them to experience stories from the characters' perspectives. Yet, even in this cutting-edge space, there's a risk of falling back on familiar tropes. The key is to understand that while technology can elevate an experience, the story itself must still capture the audience's imagination.

The hope that these new technologies could usher in a fresh wave of creativity depends on creators' willingness to embrace the unknown. Audiences are hungry for new perspectives and stories that reflect the complexities of their own lives, but too often they are served a repetitive menu of franchise leftovers. The message is clear: filmmakers need to step up and use technology to elevate their storytelling, rather than allowing it to become a shiny cover for tired ideas.

Amid the challenges, there's a flicker of hope. As we see a rising trend in independent cinema and diverse storytelling, there's a renewed interest in narratives that truly capture the richness of human experiences. Independent filmmakers are taking advantage of new technologies, sometimes on tight budgets, to craft innovative stories that resonate more deeply. These creators are willing to challenge conventions and tackle themes that mainstream studios may shy away from. Their work exemplifies the power of storytelling when paired with technological innovation, highlighting why artistic vision matters.

As audiences become more discerning, they increasingly support films that push against the norm. There's a growing desire for stories that reflect the world's diversity and complexity. Independent films like "Parasite" and "The Farewell" have struck a chord with viewers not just through their narratives but also thanks to their unique cultural viewpoints. These films show us that audiences want authenticity and originality, and they are ready to reject the sameness of formulaic tales in favor of something truly refreshing.

The film industry stands at a critical juncture. While Hollywood faces challenges such as global market shifts, franchise fatigue, and technological stagnation, it also has the opportunity for a new renaissance. The tools of innovation are right there for filmmakers to use, but it will take creative courage to break away from the familiar and explore new territories in storytelling.

As we look ahead, we should champion a cinematic world that celebrates originality, diversity, and the bold exploration of what it means to be human. By debunking the myth that technology alone can drive creativity, we can inspire a new generation of filmmakers to take the plunge into innovation. The path to revitalizing storytelling isn't just about the tools we have; it's about how we choose to use them. In a world bursting with potential, the stories waiting to be discovered are as limitless as our imaginations. It's time for filmmakers to harness technology's immense power to create narratives that reflect the richness of our shared human experience, paving the way for an era of courageous storytelling that goes beyond the boundaries of the past.

Marcus Lears

Chapter 4: The Spotify Effect: Why Music Has Stopped Evolving

In today's fast-paced digital world, where convenience is king and instant gratification shapes how we enjoy music, streaming services have emerged as the dominant force in our listening experiences. At the forefront of this revolution is Spotify, a giant that has dramatically changed how we find, share, and connect with music. While streaming has opened the door to almost limitless music options, it has also created a curious issue: despite having access to countless songs, the evolution of music itself seems to have hit a roadblock.

Picture, for a moment, the music scene of the past—an era when albums were precious treasures waiting to be explored, and artists crafted their stories with every track. Each song served as a piece of a larger puzzle, inviting us to listen closely and reflect. Fast forward to today, and the album's narrative often feels splintered. With streaming, listeners have grown accustomed to the instant satisfaction of selecting songs from playlists built by algorithms that prioritize convenience over a deeper experience. This shift prompts an important question: have we made music so easily accessible that we've unintentionally stifled creativity and innovation?

At the center of this streaming phenomenon is the rise of playlist culture. Playlists have become the go-to way for people to enjoy music, often designed to match specific moods, activities, or even tiny moments in our daily lives. While this model offers a personalized listening experience, it also comes with drawbacks. Albums—those rich musical journeys—are frequently reduced to a simple bunch of songs. Listeners tend to pick and choose tracks rather than dive into a full album, leading to a loss of the artistry that once captivated us. Instead of savoring music, we find ourselves scrolling through an endless list, each song competing for our divided attention.

In a world where playlists hold such power, artists feel the pressure to conform to market trends. The algorithm-driven nature of streaming services encourages musicians to produce singles that fit neatly into certain genres or mimic the popular sounds that currently dominate the charts. As a result, creativity often takes a back seat to the industry's demands, where catchy hooks and danceable beats overshadow the more complex musical explorations of the past. This shift has led to a safer approach in music-making, limiting the bold experimentation that once pushed artistic boundaries.

This impact of streaming goes beyond well-known artists and deeply affects newcomers too. Young musicians trying to navigate the industry today face a tough reality where success is often measured by how many streams they rack up, not necessarily by the quality of their art. The pressure to create viral hits and fit neatly into playlists sacrifices originality for commercial success, leading to a music scene where the extraordinary often fades into the background, overshadowed by the ordinary.

Additionally, the nostalgia we hold for past musical eras adds another layer of challenge to this cultural stagnation. As listeners increasingly flock to the familiar sounds of their youth—whether it's the jangly guitars of the '90s or the electronic beats of the early 2000s—there's a growing hesitation to embrace new or different sounds. Streaming platforms reinforce this trend; their algorithms are designed to suggest music that's similar to what we already enjoy, creating a comfortable bubble of familiarity. In this sea of nostalgia, new ideas struggle to break through, and the richness of fresh creativity is muffled by our affection for the past.

It's important to recognize that this stagnation isn't just about listener habits; it reflects larger corporate priorities too. The music industry has increasingly been focused on profits, and as streaming services have taken over as primary distributors, artists often find themselves caught in negotiations that prioritize financial success over their artistic vision. When decisions are made based on market research rather than genuine creativity, it raises serious concerns about the future of music as a cultural force. The essence of artistry can become overshadowed by the need for commercial success.

Interestingly, while streaming services make artists more accessible than ever, this accessibility can sometimes dampen creativity. With just a click, we can explore musicians from across the globe, yet the music that often captures our attention tends to fit a standardized mold. Having so many options doesn't always lead to a richer experience; instead, it can create a sense of disconnect from the art. The constant availability of music can make listening feel like a passive activity rather than an engaging experience with the sounds and stories that shape an artist's work.

As we navigate this ever-evolving landscape, we should take a moment to reflect on our own listening habits. Are we simply consumers of music, quickly scrolling through playlists looking for the next catchy tune? Or can we rediscover the art of truly listening— immersing ourselves in the entire experience of an album and appreciating the details that define an artist's work? By nurturing a deeper connection to music, we can start to push back against the norm and advocate for a culture that values artistic innovation over mere commercial appeal.

The impact of Spotify and similar platforms extends beyond just playlists and streaming numbers; it touches the very heart of our cultural story. The stagnation we witness raises questions about our values as both consumers and creators. How do we balance the ease of streaming with the need for new artistic expressions? How can we lift up artists who are brave enough to challenge the status quo and create something truly original? The answers lie in our choices as listeners and in the collective responsibility we share to foster a lively and varied cultural scene.

As we tackle these important questions, it becomes clear that music, in all its forms, reflects the society from which it comes. The stagnation we see isn't just an isolated issue; it's a sign of a wider cultural standstill. In a world that often prefers the familiar to the new, it's essential to support those voices that strive to break away from conventions and redefine what music can be. The future of music—and our cultural growth—hinges on our willingness to embrace the unknown, champion innovation, and engage with art that challenges our perceptions.

As we face this stagnation, we must ask ourselves: How do we reignite the creative spirit that has historically driven cultural progress? In this digital age, we need to think about how to create an environment where artistic expression can thrive, free from the constraints of commercial interests and the pull of nostalgia. The way forward may not be easy, but it requires our active involvement, a willingness to explore, and a strong commitment to pursuing creativity in all its forms. The music we choose to celebrate and uplift will ultimately shape the future of our cultural landscape, and making that choice has never been more crucial.

Playlist Culture

In today's fast-changing world of music, playlists have become a big part of how we listen. These carefully selected collections—made by both smart algorithms and creative minds—are how we discover, enjoy, and share music in the age of streaming. The playlists we come across every day not only influence what we hear but also shape what becomes popular, creating a lively mix between technology and our tastes. Playlist culture isn't just a passing trend; it's a key part of the musical scene we live in now, sparking important questions about creativity and the growth of artists.

When you think about it, playlists are like the mixtapes of our time, bringing back the excitement of discovering new music and expressing personal taste. However, today's playlists often lean heavily on data. Streaming services like Spotify use complicated algorithms to keep us engaged. These algorithms look at what songs people listen to, which tracks are popular, and many other factors to create playlists that match our preferences. The downside is that, in this setup, we often hear the same familiar songs, while fresh and new tracks can get pushed to the side.

This dependence on algorithms leads to a strange situation: even though we have access to countless music options, the music we frequently listen to is surprisingly limited. Well-known artists with established fan bases gain more exposure on these playlists, while new artists struggle to break through. For someone just starting out, like a budding musician, the challenge isn't only to make great music; they also need to find a way to get noticed enough to land on those coveted playlists. In many ways, playlists act as gatekeepers, deciding whose music gets heard while sidelining those who might not fit neatly into existing categories.

The financial side of streaming complicates things even further. With the current payment structure favoring established artists, it can be hard for new and experimental musicians to make a living. While streaming platforms promise to democratize music—giving anyone with a recording device a shot at being heard—this system often rewards what's already popular and familiar over what's new and innovative. Emerging artists find themselves in a tough spot, where the need for commercial success can overshadow their desire for creative exploration. When making money becomes the main goal, the music industry risks closing itself off from the very creativity that drives it forward.

To see how this plays out, let's think about a fictional artist named Lena. Fresh out of college, Lena has spent years perfecting her craft and playing with sounds that mix genres in her own special way. Excited to share her music, she uploads her first single to a streaming platform, hoping to connect with listeners who will appreciate her unique style. But despite her catchy and original track, Lena soon finds herself lost in the flood of new releases that pile up every day. Without the backing of a big label or support from popular playlists, her music struggles to find an audience.

As Lena faces the tough realities of the streaming world, she feels pressure to fit in with what's popular. The algorithms encourage her to make music that aligns with established genres, often pulling her away from the experimental sounds she loves. With each new song she releases, Lena wrestles with the tension between her artistic vision and the commercial demands of the industry. The frustrating irony is that her unique voice could enhance the music scene, yet the system nudges her to tone down her creativity in order to be marketable. Many artists like Lena find themselves at a crossroads, questioning if they can keep their passion alive while also meeting the demands of the industry.

The effects of playlist culture reach far beyond artists; they also affect listeners. In our playlist-driven world, we've grown used to having our music tailored to our likes. While this personalization can make listening more enjoyable, it also risks creating echo chambers where only familiar sounds play. As playlists recycle hit songs and similar artists, listeners might find themselves stuck in a loop, leading to a shared forgetfulness about the wide range of music out there. The diverse musical adventures that were once common begin to fade, replaced by a cozy familiarity with the songs we already know.

Nostalgia plays a big role in how we choose music too. Many listeners find themselves drawn to the sounds of their younger years—like 80s synth-pop or 90s grunge—which creates a loop where past hits are constantly refreshed. Streaming platforms jump on this trend, crafting playlists that remind us of our fond memories, often sidelining new and innovative music. While this cycle can be comforting, it raises a crucial question: what happens to the future of music when we keep looking back instead of embracing what's new?

As algorithms keep favoring the familiar, the music industry grapples with the harsh realities of streaming. The current royalty structure makes it harder for new artists to gain a foothold. While established stars can rake in serious cash from streaming, new acts often find it challenging to make a living. With financial success tied to metrics like monthly listeners and streams, artists often feel their worth is measured in numbers rather than the richness of their work. The paradox of this streaming era is that, while it has opened doors to music, it has also reduced artistic expression to a numbers game, where creativity can feel like a mere function of marketability.

Let's consider how this impacts genres that thrive on pushing boundaries, like jazz, avant-garde, or punk. For artists in these areas, finding an audience can be nearly impossible when major playlists often highlight commercially successful sounds. Experimental musicians who dare to challenge the norm can easily get pushed to the sidelines. Their work may resonate with a small group of fans, but the playlist algorithms focus on mainstream appeal, making it tough for them to gain the recognition their art deserves.

As we think about the effects of playlist culture, it's vital to consider how we as listeners can shape the music landscape. Are we simply passive consumers, letting algorithms make our choices for us? Or can we rediscover the joy of finding new and diverse sounds? One way to do this is by exploring music beyond the mainstream. By diving into different genres, attending local shows, following independent artists on social media, and engaging with unfamiliar sounds, we can challenge the status quo and support the kind of creativity that thrives outside of the playlist bubble.

We can also support independent artists by advocating for a fairer royalty structure that gives musicians from all backgrounds a chance to succeed. By buying music directly from artists, attending concerts, or engaging with their work on platforms that celebrate creativity over profit, we help build a cultural landscape that values innovation. This not only enriches our listening experiences but also nurtures an environment where creativity can flourish.

Ultimately, the evolution of music in the streaming age is a complex dance between technology, corporate goals, and listener habits. The playlist culture that shapes how we listen has the potential to stifle creativity, especially for new artists trying to find their place. While playlists offer undeniable convenience, we need to be aware of the downsides of algorithm-driven listening that favors the familiar over the innovative. It's our shared responsibility as listeners to push against the norm, explore the unknown, and lift up the voices that aim to redefine music.

As we continue to explore the impact of the Spotify effect, one thing stands out: the future of music and the creativity behind it depends on our openness to embracing the unfamiliar, supporting the experimental, and actively engaging with this art form. By participating in the cultural landscape, we can help shape the future of music into something vibrant, diverse, and full of possibilities, steering it away from stagnation and back toward the exciting evolution that has always been its heartbeat.

Emotional Resonance

Music has an incredible ability to spark emotions, bring back memories, and connect us to experiences we've had in the past. The songs we choose often reflect not just how we're feeling in the moment, but also the moments that have shaped who we are. This emotional connection is a big reason why we gravitate toward familiar tunes, often preferring songs we've loved for years over the latest hits. As we listen to music, that sense of nostalgia and comfort surrounds us, wrapping us in a warm hug of familiarity in a world that can often feel chaotic.

We can't overlook the psychological factors at play when we think about why we're drawn to familiar music. For many of us, specific songs are tied to certain times, places, or events in our lives. It could be the catchy chorus of a favorite 90s pop song that brings back memories of a carefree summer or the poignant melody of a ballad that reminds us of a tough breakup. These connections run deep, making it hard to resist returning to the tracks that evoke such strong feelings. Psychologist David Huron reminds us that music acts like a time machine, allowing us to revisit moments that are etched in our hearts.

In a world where change is constant, familiar music offers a touch of stability and comfort. The steady beat of a classic rock anthem or the gentle melodies from a previous era can be a source of peace when we face uncertainty. Studies show that nostalgic music can boost our sense of social connection and lift our spirits. It reminds us of shared experiences and universal feelings, serving as an emotional anchor in unpredictable times. Listening to familiar songs can calm our nerves and make us feel like we belong, reminding us that we're not alone in our journeys.

Streaming services like Spotify have tapped into this phenomenon, tailoring their algorithms to our emotional ties to music. As we listen, these algorithms analyze our preferences and suggest songs based on what we've enjoyed in the past. The result? A steady stream of nostalgia that reinforces our love for familiar sounds. This creates a feedback loop; the more we listen to nostalgic music, the more the algorithms think we want to hear those same tunes over and over. Ironically, even with a treasure trove of new music at our fingertips, we often find ourselves returning to those beloved tracks.

This cycle can keep us stuck in a musical comfort zone, making us hesitant to explore beyond what we know. It's not that we don't want to discover new music; it's just that our busy lives often lead us to seek the easiest option. With playlists designed to pull at our heartstrings, why take the time to find something new? It's clear how the comfort of familiar songs can overshadow the excitement of new discoveries.

The emotional connections we have with music also intertwine with our shared cultural memories. Certain musical eras resonate with many of us, acting as the soundtrack for significant historical moments. From the civil rights movement to the rise of feminism and the digital age, music from these times can evoke not just personal memories but also a collective sense of identity. The ability of music to capture shared emotions adds layers to our attachment to familiar sounds, as they carry the weight of history with them.

In this age of social media, the pull of nostalgia has only grown stronger. Platforms like TikTok, Instagram, and Twitter have become hotspots for reviving old songs and sparking new cultural conversations. A viral video can breathe new life into a long-forgotten track, instantly bringing it back into the spotlight. The emotional impact of these songs is heightened as they connect to visual memories shared by countless people. In this way, we become part of a larger community, united by our love for the nostalgic music of the past. This shared experience often gives us a sense of validation, reinforcing our bond with the familiar tracks we hold dear.

However, while we enjoy our nostalgic playlists, we can't overlook the challenges they pose for new and upcoming artists. In a landscape where listeners often cling to the familiar, new musicians may struggle to find their place. The emotional ties to established songs can create barriers for those trying to break through and offer something fresh. For these artists, the music scene can feel overwhelming as they compete against timeless hits that we know and love.

This challenge extends to the nature of creativity itself. Our emotional connections to the past can shape our listening habits and influence the music that gets created. If listeners primarily seek comfort and familiarity, artists might feel pressured to produce works that align with those desires. This trend could stifle the spirit of innovation that has always been at the heart of music. The rich variety of sounds that once thrived might start to fade in favor of safe, commercially successful options.

The cycle of emotional resonance, nostalgia, and comfort creates a culture where familiarity is king. The challenge we face is twofold: how do we honor the emotional connections we have with the past while still making room for new voices and fresh sounds? As listeners, we can actively strive to break free from musical routines. Seeking out new artists, attending live performances, or diving into genres we might not normally explore can help us disrupt this cycle of familiarity.

In doing so, we rediscover the joy of musical adventure. There's an exhilarating thrill in finding a song that surprises us, one that challenges our expectations and invites us to explore something completely different. By staying open to unfamiliar sounds, we not only enrich our own listening experiences but also send a welcoming message to artists that creativity is valued and encouraged.

This shift isn't just about chasing novelty for novelty's sake. It's about understanding the importance of diversity in our musical landscape. By inviting a wider range of sounds to shine, we allow music to evolve and flourish. Our cherished emotional connections can coexist alongside an openness to new experiences, creating a vibrant cultural fabric that reflects the many voices and perspectives present in our world.

Ultimately, the interplay of nostalgia and emotional resonance in today's streaming age is a complex dance. While it can offer comfort and connection, it can also lead to stagnation if we're not careful. By actively exploring new sounds and supporting artists who take risks, we can help build a culture that values both our beloved past and the exciting possibilities of the future. In doing so, we not only enrich our own musical journeys but also contribute to a thriving industry that celebrates creativity and diversity, allowing the art form we cherish to grow in meaningful ways.

Chapter 5: The Fashion Loop: Why We're Dressing Like It's 1999 (Again)

Fashion has always been a bit of a puzzle. It thrives on creativity and fresh ideas, yet it also loves to recycle styles from years gone by. It's as if fashion is stuck in a never-ending cycle, bringing back looks from the past but giving them a modern twist. Right now, we're seeing a big comeback of trends from the late 1990s, a time filled with unforgettable cultural moments and important changes in society. This revival is fueled by a fascinating mix of nostalgia, comfort, and smart marketing strategies.

To figure out why we're dressing like it's 1999 again, we need to look closely at the feelings and social dynamics involved. Nostalgia is that warm, sometimes bittersweet feeling that takes us back to a time when things seemed simpler. For many of us, it serves as a comforting escape from the craziness of today's world, reminding us of moments that, with a bit of hindsight, often feel more comforting than they really were. The late 90s were packed with memorable pop culture moments, from the hit show "Friends" to the rise of the internet, which opened up new ways to connect and share ideas. For lots of people, these memories create a sense of belonging and safety, sparking a desire to reconnect with the fashion of that time.

Nostalgia and fashion aren't just linked by sentiment; there's a deeper psychological connection too. The clothes we wear are a way to express who we are, reflecting our past experiences. When people slip into oversized flannel shirts or cargo pants that remind them of their youth, they're not just making a fashion choice; they're engaging in a conversation with their younger selves. Dressing in styles that take us back to the late 90s can feel like a time machine, allowing us to relive moments that helped shape who we are. This connection to the past can be especially comforting when life feels uncertain and chaotic.

The cultural happenings of the late 1990s played a big role in shaping the styles of that era. The internet's rise and the growth of digital culture changed how we consumed media and interacted with each other. Music videos on channels like MTV introduced new trends that quickly became staples of youth culture. The grunge movement, born in the Pacific Northwest, brought a rebellious, anti-establishment vibe marked by laid-back thrift store finds. This was a time that celebrated personal style, encouraging people to mix and match outfits in ways that felt uniquely theirs.

Figures from this time—musicians, actors, fashion designers—became icons, leaving a lasting mark on today's fashion scene. Take the Spice Girls, for example, with their vibrant take on friendship and femininity that defined a generation. Their platform shoes, colorful outfits, and bold patterns were more than just fashion statements; they symbolized empowerment and self-expression. On the flip side, Kurt Cobain's messy style, with his worn sweaters and torn jeans, resonated with a generation grappling with angst, inspiring countless followers who wanted to capture his effortless cool.

Now, as we look back at the late 90s through a modern lens, it's clear that brands have cleverly tapped into this nostalgia, eager to connect with consumers' memories. Throwback campaigns and retro-inspired collections aren't just clever marketing; they're smart strategies intended to evoke feelings of comfort and familiarity. The blend of old and new—like vintage-inspired designs made with modern materials—creates a story that resonates with shoppers seeking a link to their past while dealing with today's challenges.

Consider brands like Champion and Levi's, which have made a big comeback by leaning into nostalgic styles. They've created collections that evoke the essence of the 90s, featuring faded denim, boxy cuts, and oversized hoodies. Collaborations with influencers and celebrities only heighten the appeal of these nostalgic pieces. Social media platforms like Instagram and TikTok amplify this trend, showcasing influencers in retro looks that catch the eyes of a generation craving authenticity in the face of fast fashion.

While we enjoy this nostalgic revival, it's important to think about the impact of consumer choices shaped by corporate aims. Although it's exciting to see the return of beloved styles, we must also consider the consequences of fast fashion on our planet and the ethical questions it raises. The quick production cycles and throwaway culture of today's fashion can overshadow the true meaning behind the very styles that bring back cherished memories. The challenge is finding that sweet spot—how can we embrace the past in a way that honors its significance while also pushing for a more sustainable future?

Ultimately, the return of late 90s fashion reflects our shared feelings and experiences. The styles we choose to wear are more than just trends; they signal a longing for connection and a desire to revisit moments that shaped our younger years. As we navigate this cyclical nature of fashion, it becomes clear that the themes of nostalgia, identity, and consumerism are all intertwined. By understanding these elements, we can appreciate not just the clothes we choose, but the stories they carry and the memories they spark. Fashion isn't just about looking good; it's about feeling good, reconnecting with the past, and celebrating the vibrant, chaotic beauty of life itself.

Fast Fashion Impact

The fast fashion world is a whirlwind of excitement and confusion, where the rush to stay trendy often squashes the very heart of creativity. This industry thrives on speed and low prices, putting profits ahead of real artistry and sustainability. In this fast-paced environment, economic pressures create a never-ending craving for something new, leading to a system that seems designed for quick profits rather than thoughtful design. The end result? A fashion industry that's stuck on a merry-go-round of fleeting trends, leaving little space for the unique styles that once made fashion an art.

At its core, fast fashion revolves around a straightforward yet powerful idea: get trendy clothing to consumers in record time and at rock-bottom prices. Brands accomplish this through a complicated web of production and distribution that puts efficiency above everything else. They employ a method called "just-in-time" manufacturing, which allows them to respond to trends almost instantly. By keeping a close eye on social media, runway shows, and celebrity fashion, companies can figure out what's popular and rush to create similar items, often before the original trend has fully developed. This approach not only strips away the deep creativity involved in true fashion design but also reduces style to simple numbers on a chart.

The economic motivations behind fast fashion create an environment where quantity trumps quality. Designers find themselves in a never-ending cycle, forced to produce new collections at a dizzying pace—sometimes every few weeks—to satisfy consumer demand. This has led to the idea of "trend cycles," where fashion becomes a whirlwind of quickly changing styles that often borrow heavily from the past. Instead of encouraging originality, brands tend to recycle old ideas, resulting in a landscape filled with echoes of what used to be popular rather than fresh takes on fashion. It's ironic: while the industry likes to see itself as cutting-edge, it often relies on trends that have already come and gone, recycling them with little to no innovation.

Take a moment to think about how brands now often prefer quick imitations over real design. For example, when a popular clothing line launches a collection inspired by a viral moment, they might choose to reinterpret what's already out there instead of investing time and resources into creating something new. This leads to a fashion environment overflowing with familiar shapes and styles— each version feeling more like a copy than an evolution of fashion. As a result, shoppers are met with a parade of options that, while abundant, lack true creativity.

The fast pace of trend cycles is even more intensified by how consumers behave today. With platforms like Instagram and TikTok making fashion so accessible, there's a growing demand for constant newness. Shoppers aren't just sitting back and watching; they're actively engaging in the fashion conversation, excitedly posting their own takes on trends and hunting for the next big thing. This endless thirst for novelty fuels the fast fashion engine, driving brands to pump out even more versions of what's already popular— often sacrificing originality in the process. When every new piece of clothing is just a rehash of something that's already been done, it becomes tougher for genuine innovation to take hold.

Amid this whirlwind of consumption, it's important to think about the environmental and ethical issues tied to fast fashion. The industry's relentless drive for speed and cheap prices has sparked serious sustainability concerns that we can't overlook. Producing inexpensive clothing often comes at a huge environmental toll, with factories causing pollution and waste on a massive scale. Water use, chemical runoff, and throwing clothes into landfills are just a few of the urgent problems linked to fast fashion's production habits. Many of us, as consumers, are left facing the uncomfortable truth that our love for affordable clothing is part of a much larger environmental crisis.

Additionally, the ethical side of fast fashion is equally troubling. The push for lower prices frequently leads to exploitative labor practices in poorer countries, where workers endure long hours and receive minimal pay just to meet the demands of rapid production. As brands look to save on costs, the human side of fashion is often ignored, leaving behind workers who are frequently paid less than what they need to survive. This creates a tough situation for consumers, who feel torn between wanting trendy clothes and grappling with the ethical consequences of their purchases.

As fast fashion keeps expanding, we must ask ourselves: can we reimagine this industry in a way that respects creativity, sustainability, and ethical production? Some brands are starting to shift gears, exploring slow fashion movements that advocate for handcrafted designs, quality over quantity, and a more mindful approach to shopping. These initiatives encourage consumers to invest in pieces that are not only stylish but also made with care for both the environment and the people involved in their creation.

While the appeal of fast fashion is strong, it's vital for shoppers to acknowledge the influence they have in shaping the industry. Changing our buying habits can send a powerful message to brands, urging them to adopt more sustainable practices and focus on true creativity. This calls for a readiness to step away from the fast fashion cycle, resisting the temptation for instant gratification in favor of more thoughtful choices.

In a world where trends keep getting recycled, we have the chance to adopt a more conscious approach to fashion. By choosing originality over imitation, consumers can push the industry to champion creativity, sustainability, and ethics. Fashion can be more than just a reflection of our current times; it can be a driver of change—a way to celebrate the past while paving a new path forward. Embracing this mindset allows us to reclaim fashion as an art form, celebrating the creativity that inspires, uplifts, and connects us all.

Social Media Influence

In a world where the vibrant streets of Milan and Paris compete with the dazzling screens of our smartphones, social media has become a powerful force in shaping fashion. Platforms like Instagram and TikTok have transformed from simple online hangouts into the main stages for fashion today, where new trends are born, celebrated, and sometimes forgotten just as quickly. Their influence reaches far beyond the digital world, affecting how we shop and what we consider stylish. Social media is, in many ways, rewriting the rules of fashion.

Think about Instagram for a moment. With its carefully curated feeds and endless scroll of eye-catching images, it has changed how we see and interact with fashion. Here, the visuals take the spotlight, and every post is like a tribute to what's hot. Influencers, with their stunning selfies and perfectly styled outfits, have become the new gatekeepers of fashion. They hold immense power over what consumers choose to buy. With just a simple swipe, they can launch a brand into fame or lead it to a quick downfall.

This trend is not just for the established names in fashion; even a teenager filming a TikTok video in her bedroom can suddenly kick off a new trend. Styles that used to take months or even years to develop can now appear overnight, driven by viral challenges and hashtags. We watch as users recreate these viral moments, leading to a whirlwind of imitation that can overshadow true creativity.

But this fast-paced world of fashion trends comes with its own set of challenges. The focus on aesthetics often pushes for recognizable and "safe" choices over bold creativity. Social media algorithms tend to promote visually appealing content, meaning that what gets the most likes and shares often drives what brands and individuals present. As a result, fashion risks becoming a popularity contest, leaving originality on the sidelines.

It's ironic that the very platforms aimed at making fashion accessible can actually stifle personal expression. As users shape their feeds to fit the latest trends, they may find themselves stuck in a cycle that discourages them from trying new things. The pressure to conform to social media's beauty standards can lead to a homogenization of style, where the same outfits pop up on various profiles, dulling the uniqueness that fashion once cherished. Instead of showcasing personal flair, the scene can turn into a display of sameness, reducing fashion to a game of catch-up.

Let's take a closer look at influencers within this context. Many have mastered the art of presenting fashion as more than just clothing; it's a lifestyle. They often promote partnerships with brands, blending sponsored content into their feeds while trying to maintain an aura of authenticity. While this can build trust among followers, it also raises questions about the originality of what we're seeing. Are we witnessing unique styles, or is this just a clever marketing strategy designed to make the most of social media's reach?

For many shoppers, the urge to mimic influencers can feel overwhelming. When an outfit's worth can be judged by its social media presence, it affects how people view their own wardrobes. The strive for a "perfect" look, as portrayed on Instagram or TikTok, can lead to feelings of inadequacy. When personal style is reduced to the number of likes and shares, it takes away the joy of expressing oneself. Instead of exploring colors, shapes, and textures, many focus on following the paths laid out by popular influencers, which stifles innovation.

The viral nature of social media only adds to the problem. Trends can skyrocket to fame overnight, pushing everyone to rush to copy what's trending. While this fosters a sense of community—everyone sporting the latest "it" item—the relentless urge to keep up can make it hard to be authentic. Rather than developing their unique style, many end up buying the latest craze without really knowing what they like versus what they think they should like.

As we navigate the flood of social media content, it's also worth considering how these platforms contribute to the commercialization of fashion. Brands are often eager to jump on viral trends, quickly producing knock-offs of popular styles. This rapid reproduction means that true design often gets lost in the chaos. The focus shifts from creative exploration to commercial gain, where the need to stay trendy overshadows the value of thoughtful design.

Additionally, social media can perpetuate unrealistic beauty standards and ideals about fashion. As users scroll through a seemingly endless stream of perfect images, it becomes harder to appreciate one's own body type, style, and preferences. The constant barrage of filtered photos can warp our views of what's beautiful, leading people to make choices that align with narrow social media definitions instead of celebrating their own identities.

This cycle of imitation and idealization can further alienate those who don't fit the mold, making them question their own fashion choices. Personal aesthetics become tied to social acceptance, where individuals feel pressured to shape their identities around what's popular rather than what resonates with them. The once colorful world of fashion can start to feel like an echo chamber, where authentic voices struggle to be heard.

Yet, within this complicated landscape, there's a spark of hope. The same social media platforms that can restrict creativity also have the potential to drive change and innovation. As more people become aware of the limitations imposed by social media standards, a counter-movement is starting to take shape. Individuals are reclaiming their unique styles, sharing their personal stories, and celebrating the beauty found in imperfections. More and more, we're seeing a rise in "real" fashion—a movement that champions individuality over conformity, focusing on the unique stories that each outfit tells.

Creators are stepping away from the polished perfection often showcased on social media to reveal their authentic experiences. They're challenging traditional beauty standards and redefining what it means to be stylish. Whether it's through sustainable fashion efforts, thrifting, or upcycling, users are increasingly embracing a narrative centered on creativity, authenticity, and self-expression.

This shift could reshape the future of fashion, empowering individuals to make choices that feel true to themselves instead of simply following trends. By valuing authenticity and embracing diverse styles, the industry can move past the superficiality often promoted by social media. We can begin to celebrate individuality and the stories behind each piece of clothing.

However, this change requires teamwork. Brands, influencers, and consumers all need to challenge the norm and prioritize true creativity over fleeting trends. By embracing sustainable practices, supporting independent designers, and nurturing a culture of experimentation, the fashion industry can regain its innovative spirit. It's about changing the focus from being driven by trends to being guided by personal style, where self-expression takes the lead.

The connection between social media and fashion is complex, filled with both opportunities and challenges. As we move through this digital space, we need to be aware of the influences shaping our choices. By encouraging a culture that values authenticity and celebrates unique styles, we can create a fashion world that's vibrant and diverse—one where creativity thrives and everyone can express themselves.

In this ongoing conversation about fashion, we should remember that while social media can be a platform for self-expression, it shouldn't control our sense of style. By embracing our true selves and stepping beyond the limits of social validation, we can enter a future where fashion isn't just about following trends but about sharing our stories. It's time to take back the narrative, to celebrate the art of personal style, and to let creativity flourish in all the right places.

Marcus Lears

Chapter 6: Social Media Echo Chambers: The Death of Subculture

Subcultures have always been the bold outsiders in our cultural world, bursting out from the cracks of mainstream society. They capture the spirit of defiance, marked by their distinct values, styles, and, most importantly, their sense of belonging. From the raw energy of punk rock in dimly lit clubs to the exhilarating vibe of skateboarding, these subcultures provide a refuge for those who feel like they don't fit in with the polished, uniform aspects of popular culture. At their heart, they celebrate individuality, turn their backs on conformity, and create a space for self-expression.

To really grasp how these vibrant movements have developed, we first need to figure out what exactly makes a subculture. Subcultures are groups that showcase unique traits that set them apart from the larger cultural landscape. They thrive on shared interests, styles, and values that blend into a collective identity. Look at the punk rock scene from the late 1970s and early 1980s. It sprang up as a raw response to the excesses of mainstream rock and the political climate of the time. Punk was more than just music; it was a mindset—challenging social norms, critiquing consumerism, and embracing a DIY (do-it-yourself) attitude. The look was just as vital, with ripped jeans, vibrant hairstyles, and an attitude that practically shouted rebellion.

In a similar vein, skateboarding culture that emerged in the 1980s embodies this same spirit. It began on the streets and in empty swimming pools of California, representing a lifestyle centered around freedom, creativity, and a strong sense of community among skaters. The friendships formed in skate parks crossed different backgrounds, uniting people with a shared love for the thrill of skating. Both punk and skateboarding created a feeling of belonging, nurturing a close-knit community where creativity could thrive without the limits placed by mainstream acceptance.

However, as we look through the history of these subcultures, we can't ignore a concerning change. The very qualities that made them powerful and unique are starting to fade under the pressure of commodification. The heart of this shift lies in how social media platforms have made it easier to market these once-unique communities. Platforms like Instagram and TikTok, which initially provided a space for connection and expression, have unintentionally taken on the role of cultural gatekeepers, shaping and controlling what is seen as 'cool' or 'trendy.'

Take the rise of vintage clothing, which stems from the thrifting community that grew as a sustainable option against fast fashion. Once a niche for fashion enthusiasts who thrived on the excitement of searching for unique finds, it has been taken over by social media influencers eager to profit from the aesthetic. What started as a lifestyle grounded in sustainability and individuality has morphed into a marketable trend, filled with perfectly curated Instagram feeds and sponsored posts that focus more on brand names than the stories behind the pieces. The essence of thrift culture, which once celebrated reusing and recycling, gets drowned out by the constant push for consumerism, where the joy of discovering a rare item gets swapped for its commodified version, stripped of context and authenticity.

The effects of commodification reach far beyond the looks of vintage clothing. The flood of branded merchandise and corporate sponsorships dilutes the core messages of subcultures, making them easy targets for appropriation and misrepresentation. When entities that once boldly stood against mainstream culture become marketable products, the tension that once fueled their existence disappears. The punk attitude of rebellion turns into a fashion statement, its raw energy transformed into trendy clothing lines. Skateboarding, an underground movement that once celebrated risk and innovation, is now polished and plastered in corporate ads aimed at profits rather than fostering true connections with the culture.

This trend of commodification spills into many areas of creativity. Music, art, and even language, which used to be tools for subcultural identity, are frequently co-opted by corporations eager to cash in on their popularity. Festivals once dedicated to celebrating underground movements are saturated with corporate sponsors, turning them into massive marketing events that prioritize brand visibility over genuine experiences. The real connections formed in these environments are replaced by carefully designed marketing strategies that aim to boost consumer engagement, chipping away at the very foundations that made these subcultures matter in the first place.

As we navigate this complex world, it's important to listen to the voices of cultural theorists and sociologists who have studied the impacts of commodification. Thinkers like Herbert Marcuse have warned that commodifying culture leads to a "one-dimensional" existence, where true creativity and human expression are sidelined in favor of what can be sold. Marcuse's insights feel particularly relevant today, in a digital age where social media algorithms decide what is popular and, by extension, what gets recognized.

Similarly, sociologist David Hesmondhalgh points out how cultural commodification results in a homogenization of culture, where diversity and authenticity are lost. As subcultures get turned into commodities, their unique features often get smoothed out to create a product that can be sold to the masses. The result? A culture that lacks the richness and depth of what came before, reduced to fleeting trends that quickly fade from our memories. When every niche movement can be distilled into a marketable item, we risk losing the vibrant mix that once flourished.

Moreover, commodifying subcultures weakens the communal bonds that are often central to their existence. Where once people came together to share experiences and forge connections, the influx of commercial interests breeds competition and individualism. The sense of community that formed the backbone of these subcultures gets eroded by the relentless chase for profit, leading to a culture where authenticity is sacrificed for consumerism.

Given these insights, it's vital to recognize the overarching forces driving the commodification of subcultures. The allure of social media, with its promise of visibility and approval, can often be more of a double-edged sword than a blessing. While it allows subcultures to gain recognition and share their messages, it also leaves them vulnerable to the very forces that aim to commercialize and dilute their essence. As individuals navigate this space, finding a balance between embracing opportunities offered by new technologies and protecting the authenticity that defines subcultures becomes essential.

When we think about the commodification of subcultures, we also need to consider the question of agency. While social media's influence is significant, individuals still hold the power to shape their own stories and resist the urge to commodify. By critically assessing their consumption habits and challenging the narratives pushed by corporate interests, people can reclaim their agency in this new cultural landscape. This means actively seeking out and supporting grassroots movements that value authenticity over profit, and engaging with art, music, and ideas that arise from real-life experiences rather than commercial frameworks.

As we reflect on the commodification of subcultures, we find ourselves at an important juncture. The ongoing struggle between authenticity and commodification reminds us of how fragile cultural movements can be when faced with market forces. If we want to protect the unique identities that subcultures provide, we need to be mindful of our consumption habits, demand transparency from the brands we choose to support, and prioritize genuine connections with those who share our love for creative expression. Only then can we hope to revive the innovative spirit that once thrived underground, allowing subcultures to grow anew in ways that honor their roots while navigating the challenges of a rapidly changing cultural landscape.

Homogenization through Virality

In our world filled with clicks, likes, shares, and retweets, the idea of going viral carries both excitement and concern. Social media can send a funny meme or a touching video soaring into the spotlight, reaching millions within hours. But in this race for attention, something truly valuable is often lost—depth, originality, and cultural significance. When we think about virality in the context of social media, it's not just about getting noticed; it's about sharing experiences that often come at the expense of individual expression and the rich diversity of our cultures.

To really grasp how virality works, we first need to understand what it means in the realm of social media. Essentially, it's content that spreads quickly because of user engagement, fueled by algorithms designed to highlight what gets the most views and reactions. These algorithms tend to prioritize sensational content over more thoughtful pieces, resulting in a digital world filled with trends that, while entertaining, often flatten the vibrant diversity of human culture into bite-sized snippets.

Take a moment to think about the viral dance challenges we see on platforms like TikTok. One minute, a catchy song is playing, and the next, millions are joining in to replicate the dance, sharing their own takes on it. This rapid spread of a single trend often overshadows the original context. The unique style of the choreographer and the deeper meaning behind the song fade into the background, while the immediate entertainment takes center stage. It's a culture of imitation that dilutes the original message, leaving viewers with a polished version of creativity that's easy to consume but lacks real substance.

The nature of viral trends creates a cycle that favors copying over creativity. Many creators feel the need to hop on the latest trend, often losing sight of their own unique voices in the process. The pressure to make content that fits the current style or narrative can stifle original ideas, leading many to recycle familiar concepts instead of exploring new ones. For example, a quirky recipe that captures the public's interest can inspire countless variations; yet, in a flood of similar dishes, the original spark of creativity might get lost. The cook's personal story gets buried beneath the wave of imitation, turning what was once a true expression into just another item on the viral menu.

This trend of homogenization isn't limited to food and dance; it seeps into all forms of cultural expression. Memes that once conveyed specific humor or social commentary often lose their context and get mass-produced, draining them of their original impact. A clever, localized joke can quickly become a global sensation, highlighting how virality tends to erase cultural differences and turn everything into a uniform product. The genuine laughter that comes from shared experiences is replaced with a generic chuckle that fails to connect on a deeper level.

The psychological effects of this homogenization are also significant. For many creators, the relentless pursuit of virality can lead to burnout and anxiety. The constant need to stay on top of trends fosters a culture of insecurity, where success is measured by how quickly one can adapt to or imitate what's popular. The fear of being left behind can overshadow the joy of creating, resulting in a stressful environment that values fleeting fame over true artistic expression.

To illustrate this, think about the experiences of people involved in various subcultures who feel pressured to conform to viral trends. Many express their worries about losing their unique identities in this process. A street artist, for example, might find their work going viral on Instagram, but instead of feeling celebrated, they face a flood of imitations that dilute their original message. The excitement of sharing a genuine piece of art shifts to frustration as they watch others replicate their style without grasping its deeper meaning. These stories often highlight a sense of disconnection amid their newfound visibility, underscoring the emotional strain of navigating a landscape that favors copying over individuality.

The algorithms that drive virality play a big role in shaping this scenario. They operate on the principle of engagement, promoting content that gets strong reactions—be it laughter, anger, or awe. Unfortunately, this algorithm-driven approach often sidelines nuanced content that requires more thought or emotional connection. As a result, creators who dare to tackle complex ideas or challenge societal norms may find their work overlooked in favor of more sensational, easier-to-digest pieces. This creates an environment where louder voices dominate, drowning out those who offer more thoughtful or challenging viewpoints.

This raises an important question: what happens to the cultural significance of original content in the fast-paced world of trends? As viral moments become commercialized and mainstream, they can lose their local or cultural roots. The rich histories, traditions, and struggles that inform these expressions often get lost along the way. For example, a dance rooted in a specific culture may lose its meaning as it gets reinterpreted for a wider audience, ultimately diminishing the heritage it represents. In the relentless chase for virality, the authenticity that once gave these expressions life is sacrificed for mass appeal.

While this homogenization might seem like a side effect of the digital age, it actually reflects a broader societal trend that values surface-level engagement over meaningful connections. The relationships formed through shared interests in subcultures risk being replaced by transactional interactions that prioritize popularity over authenticity. Instead of nurturing deep connections based on shared values and experiences, social media often promotes a culture of competition, where creators seek validation through numbers rather than genuine interactions.

As we navigate this complicated web of virality, it becomes clear how high the stakes are. The cultural landscape we explore today is filled with challenges that threaten to erase the unique voices and stories that enhance our society. The homogenization of culture through viral trends can lead to a loss of diversity that ultimately impoverishes our collective human experience. As we engage with content, we need to remain aware, recognizing the importance of originality and the unique stories behind these trends.

In this light, the responsibility lies not just with creators but also with audiences. By actively seeking out diverse voices and supporting those who challenge the norm, we can help create an environment that values authenticity and innovation. Engaging with content that pushes boundaries and invites deeper conversations can provide an alternative to the culture of replication.

Moreover, it's vital for social media platforms to reflect on their influence in shaping the cultural landscape. While algorithms aim to maximize engagement, they also need to consider the consequences of their choices in what gets promoted. Finding a balance between virality and authenticity can lead to a healthier ecosystem where diverse expressions are celebrated rather than overshadowed by mainstream trends.

Ultimately, our journey through the world of virality points to a pressing need for a cultural revival—one that respects the complexities of the human experience and cherishes the many expressions that arise from our diverse identities. As we navigate this digital landscape, we must foster a culture that prioritizes depth over superficiality, encouraging creativity that resonates with the heart of what it means to be human. Only then can we hope to preserve the richness of subcultures and ensure that their voices continue to be heard in a world increasingly defined by the fleeting nature of virality.

Monetization of Culture

Social media has changed our lives in many ways, but perhaps one of the biggest shifts has been the rise of influencers. These individuals aren't just celebrities; they often represent specific subcultures, acting as bridges between their communities and big businesses. In a world driven by likes, shares, and followers, influencers have become powerful figures who can set trends and change norms. However, with this spotlight comes significant pressure. The temptation to make money has led to a tricky balancing act between staying true to one's self and catering to commercial interests, raising important questions about the cultures they represent.

It's hard to ignore that influencers, while celebrated for their creativity and relatable content, often play a crucial role in the cultural exchange between subcultures and brands. Companies quickly recognize how influencers can connect with audiences in ways that traditional advertising can't. They take advantage of the trust and authenticity these influencers offer, making it difficult to tell where genuine engagement ends and paid promotion begins. For instance, when an influencer shows off a punk-inspired outfit, they might be seen as a true representative of that scene. But once that outfit is featured in a sponsored post from a major retailer, the story changes. What began as a form of self-expression can turn into just another marketing tactic, often losing its original meaning in the process.

There are many examples of brands adopting subcultural styles without any real understanding of their roots. Take streetwear, for example. It sprang from the gritty vibe of urban culture, known for its rebellious spirit and authenticity. But as luxury brands started to enter the scene—often hiring influencers with little connection to the original movement—things began to feel off. A limited-edition sneaker from an upscale fashion house, promoted by an influencer with millions of followers, feels miles away from streetwear's grassroots beginnings. The culture is turned into a product, stripped of its social messages and rebellious heart.

The ethical concerns that arise from such practices deserve careful thought. Authenticity is the heartbeat of any subculture, and if it's misrepresented, it can lead to backlash from community members who feel their identities are being exploited. When a brand profits from a subculture without truly understanding it, they risk alienating the very people who built and nurtured that culture. This issue is particularly visible in the punk music scene, where logos and imagery are commodified and sold on t-shirts, often endorsed by influencers who don't appreciate the music's socio-political roots. Many in the punk community voice their frustration, feeling that their values have been hijacked for profit, reducing a rich cultural movement to a series of fashion statements.

However, the responsibility doesn't lie solely with corporations. Creators often find themselves caught in a confusing position, torn between wanting to make money from their work and holding on to their artistic integrity. This struggle—between being a creator and becoming a product—is something many influencers experience. On one side, there's the lure of financial support that could open the door to more artistic freedom. On the other, there's the fear of losing what makes their work special. The question remains: can someone truly thrive as an artist in a world that increasingly demands they conform to commercial standards?

Consider an artist who starts sharing their unique music on platforms like Instagram and TikTok. Their fresh sound draws in thousands of fans, leading to opportunities for sponsorships and brand collaborations. At first, the artist sees this as a chance to elevate their craft. But as the offers pile up, so does the pressure to meet brand expectations. They find themselves at a crossroads, conflicted between creating for self-expression and producing content that caters to commercial interests. The outcome? Their once-authentic music starts to sound like a formulaic version of what's seen as marketable. What resonated with their followers begins to fade, replaced by a product designed to sell.

This issue isn't limited to the music industry. It echoes through various forms of creative expression. Visual artists, dancers, and writers are all faced with similar pressures, prompting them to question the sustainability of making a living from their art. The act of creating can become tangled with financial survival, which can stifle innovation. The chase for income can sometimes dilute the deep connection to their work, turning a vibrant creative journey into a calculated strategy for making money.

The tension between staying true to one's artistic vision and the pressures of financial success reflects a larger trend in society. As creators navigate the world of social media, they confront the tough truth that making money often comes with sacrifices. The desire for validation can mix with the need to stay afloat financially, pushing many artists to chase trends instead of carving out their own paths. The risk here is a culture that values conformity over creativity. Those who dare to challenge the status quo might find their work overshadowed by more mainstream, commercially appealing content.

The commodification of culture highlights how fragile authenticity can be. Subcultures, rich with history and significance, can easily be reduced to mere marketing tools when caught up in the whirlwind of social media monetization. This situation raises important questions: who really gets to tell the stories of these subcultures? Are influencers the true voice of the culture, or just players in a script written by corporations? When the original creators are sidelined in the quest for profits, the intricate fabric of culture starts to unravel.

Moreover, this commodification isn't just about influencers; it extends to the platforms that showcase their content. Social media algorithms often favor popular and commercially driven content over more nuanced and genuine expressions. This creates a cycle where the loudest voices, usually backed by corporate sponsorship, dominate the conversation. As those on the margins struggle to be heard, the unique contributions of subcultures risk being overshadowed, leading to a one-dimensional view of cultural diversity.

It's also important to recognize that while the commercialization of culture brings challenges, it can also create new opportunities. Crowdfunding platforms, for example, allow creators to connect directly with their audiences, sidestepping traditional gatekeepers. By building a sense of community and shared investment, artists can maintain more control over their work. This approach encourages a more authentic relationship between creators and consumers, prioritizing genuine engagement over simple transactions.

In the end, the monetization of culture presents a complex challenge that requires careful consideration. As creators look for financial support, they must stay aware of the risks involved. Finding a balance between artistic freedom and economic viability is tricky and calls for reflection on what it means to be an artist in a world that increasingly leans toward commercialization. The push and pull between authenticity and profit will keep shaping our cultural landscape, encouraging both creators and audiences to engage thoughtfully with what's at stake.

For audiences, their role is just as critical. By intentionally supporting artists who value authenticity over mere popularity, they can help shape the future of cultural expression. A thoughtful viewer can seek out content that resonates on a deeper level, fostering an environment where originality is celebrated rather than stifled. Engaging with art that challenges norms and invites exploration can cultivate a cultural ecosystem that values diversity and depth.

Ultimately, the monetization of culture is a complicated dance between authenticity and capitalism, with influencers at the heart of this ongoing conversation. As the landscape keeps changing, it's crucial for creators to move through this space with intention, staying true to their roots while seeking ways to grow sustainably. At the same time, audiences must become active participants in the cultural dialogue, advocating for voices and expressions that honor the rich histories and identities of subcultures. By nurturing a culture that prioritizes authenticity over commodification, we can contribute to a vibrant and diverse creative world, one that respects the roots of cultural movements while embracing new possibilities ahead.

Marcus Lears

Chapter 7: The Consolidation Crisis: Big Tech and the Death of Diversity

In today's world, where everything seems connected and our lives are increasingly digital, it's surprising to see how a handful of big tech companies hold so much power over our culture. As we scroll through social media or binge-watch our favorite shows, we might feel like we're part of a lively and varied cultural scene. But beneath this surface, there's a concerning truth: the creation and sharing of culture is controlled by just a few major players. The platforms that deliver our entertainment often shape the content in ways that limit the voices and stories we get to hear.

At the center of this issue are the giants of Big Tech—Amazon, Google, and Facebook. These companies have shifted from simply sharing information and products to becoming the gatekeepers of our cultural experience. With their massive resources and smart algorithms, they don't just influence what we watch or read; they also decide what gets created in the first place. It can feel like the conversation around culture has been handed over to a small group of tech leaders who make decisions based on data rather than imagination.

Take Amazon, for example. Once celebrated for changing the retail landscape, it has now grown into a powerhouse in entertainment through Amazon Prime Video. But this shift isn't just about making life easier for viewers. Amazon uses its vast customer data to produce shows and films that are calculated to succeed, often ignoring innovative or unconventional stories that don't fit its established patterns. In this environment, taking creative risks isn't encouraged, leading to a sea of programming that relies on familiar plots and characters instead of offering fresh and diverse stories. Unique perspectives that once thrived in independent film and television are increasingly pushed to the sidelines, as content that appeals to the broadest audience takes precedence.

Similarly, Google plays a huge role in shaping what we see and value in culture. As the leading search engine and a major player in online advertising through YouTube, Google changes how we consume content. Creators often feel pressured to make clickbait videos that emphasize shock value over real substance, resulting in a flood of similar content that targets the lowest common denominator. Google's algorithms essentially control what information we receive, guiding public discussions in a way that favors mainstream views while leaving smaller, niche voices unheard. This focus on popular content not only limits diversity but also creates an echo chamber where only the loudest voices are amplified, overshadowing more thoughtful or dissenting opinions.

Facebook has transformed social media into a powerful tool for sharing content, but it does so with a major drawback. Its algorithms are designed to boost user engagement by prioritizing exciting and often inflammatory posts. This creates a culture of outrage that can lower the quality of conversations. Just like a runaway train, Facebook's system favors dramatic posts that generate likes, shares, and comments, making calmer, more reflective contributions nearly invisible. This affects more than just social interactions; it shapes what we collectively understand and know by narrowing the range of what we can see and discuss.

This centralization isn't just about convenience; it deeply affects cultural diversity and innovation. When fewer companies control the storytelling and creation of cultural content, we risk losing the richness of human experiences to profit-driven motives. Smaller creators and independent voices struggle to gain attention in a system that favors established brands and franchises. The result is a stagnation of ideas, as we see the same themes and narratives recycled over and over again, leaving less room for fresh perspectives that could invigorate our culture.

Look at the music industry, for example, where consolidation hampers artistic expression. With major labels controlling the distribution channels, many new artists find it nearly impossible to get their music heard. This leads to a situation where the same mainstream hits dominate the charts, drowning out innovative sounds and new genres that could thrive in a more diverse environment. Independent labels and artists are left trying to navigate a system that prioritizes what's already popular, which limits their chances to share their creativity and reach potential fans.

The impact stretches to literature, too. As publishing houses consolidate under economic pressures, many unique voices struggle to find a place in the literary world. Publishers often lean towards well-known bestsellers and easily marketable stories, leaving a significant gap in the types of books available. Readers miss out on the richness that comes from a variety of voices and experiences. When cultural production is so tightly controlled, we end up with a limited selection that doesn't represent the full range of human experience, stifling empathy and understanding along the way.

As we reflect on the broader effects of this cultural centralization, we should also think about how our own choices might be fueling this cycle. In a time when convenience is king, many of us unintentionally contribute to the concentration of cultural power. It's just so easy to access content from a single source, which can lead to a narrow view of culture. We often consume only what's right in front of us, ignoring alternative stories that could offer new insights or experiences. In doing so, we reinforce a system that favors sameness over diversity, deepening the very issues we criticize.

To create a more vibrant cultural landscape, we all need to make a conscious effort and be active participants. This means examining our consumption habits and seeking out alternatives. Whether it's watching independent films, reading books by diverse authors, or supporting local music scenes, there are countless ways to push back against the forces of centralization. By looking for underrepresented and unconventional voices, we can help build a cultural environment that values variety and creativity instead of uniformity.

As we navigate a world dominated by a few tech giants, we must remember that we still have the power to shape culture, even if it feels scattered right now. It's up to each of us—consumers, creators, and advocates—to support diversity and innovation in our cultural landscape, challenging the norm and reminding ourselves that true creativity flourishes when a multitude of voices are allowed to thrive. By taking action, we can reclaim the cultural story from the grips of centralization and breathe new life into the creative ecosystem that desperately needs it.

Through our collective efforts, we can open the door to a new era of innovation and variety, ensuring that future generations inherit a cultural landscape filled with diversity, creativity, and expression. The future of our culture is at stake, and it's our responsibility to tip the scales in favor of the many unique voices that are waiting to be heard.

Media Ownership

The world of media ownership has changed a lot over the past few decades. What used to be a vibrant mix of independent voices has now turned into a tightly controlled space dominated by just a few big corporations. This shift has major effects on the stories we tell, the voices we hear, and the cultural narratives that define our society. When we look at how media ownership has evolved over time, it becomes clear that the mergers and acquisitions haven't just created larger media companies; they have also significantly limited the diversity of creative expression available to us all.

Let's take a closer look at some important players in this ongoing story of consolidation. In the early days of media, we saw a surge of creative outlets. Independent film studios, small publishing houses, and local radio stations flourished, each adding their own unique perspective to the cultural conversation. But as time went on, things began to change. Big corporations recognized that media and entertainment could be lucrative, leading to a series of mergers that reshaped the creative landscape forever. A prime example of this is Disney's acquisition of 21st Century Fox in 2019. This deal, worth more than $71 billion, wasn't just a financial transaction—it marked a significant change in the types of stories available to us.

By acquiring Fox, Disney greatly expanded its influence in the media world, bringing a wealth of content—including the beloved Fox film library, various TV networks, and production studios—under its control. The immediate result of this consolidation was a noticeable decrease in the variety of narratives in the marketplace. With Disney now a major player, the range of stories and ideas started to shrink. Franchises like Star Wars, Marvel, and Pixar began to dominate the conversation, while independent filmmakers and alternative narratives struggled to get noticed. Consequently, we're often left with a narrow selection of stories that tend to cater to existing fan bases, rather than exploring new and innovative themes.

To highlight this trend, let's take a look at some numbers regarding media ownership concentration. Back in the 1980s, there were over fifty companies producing television and film content in the United States. Fast forward to today, and that number has dropped significantly, with just six conglomerates—Comcast, Disney, AT&T, ViacomCBS, Sony, and Netflix—now controlling most of what we watch and read. This concentration of power is troubling because it means fewer voices are shaping the narratives that fill our culture.

The effects of this trend go beyond just numbers; they touch on the very fabric of our society. When a small group of corporations has so much power over media content, the stories we see and hear start to reflect their interests instead of the rich variety of experiences found in our population. This leads to cultural stagnation, where creative and groundbreaking ideas struggle to find a space. Instead, we often find ourselves bombarded with a repetitive cycle of sequels, remakes, and reboots that reinforce existing narratives instead of challenging or expanding them.

The decline of independent media is particularly concerning, as it goes hand-in-hand with the rise of corporate giants. Independent filmmakers and content creators frequently face huge obstacles in a landscape dominated by a few main players. Many independent films struggle to find distribution, and the creators behind them often lack the resources to compete with the marketing budgets of major studios. Because of this, unique voices and fresh perspectives can easily be overlooked, resulting in a public discourse that doesn't reflect the rich diversity of the world around us.

In conversations with independent filmmakers, the sense of frustration is unmistakable. One filmmaker shared, "It feels like we're always fighting an uphill battle. You pour your heart and soul into a project only to find that it's nearly impossible to get it seen. The big players have the marketing power, and it's disheartening when you know your work could resonate with audiences if only they had the chance to see it." These feelings are echoed by many creators who feel sidelined in a system that favors established franchises over innovative storytelling.

The impact of concentrated media ownership doesn't stop with film and television; the music industry has also faced significant consolidation, with major labels controlling distribution channels, leaving independent artists struggling to make a name for themselves. With fewer labels willing to take a chance on unique sounds, the charts tend to be dominated by a small number of mainstream hits, which stifles artistic expression and innovation.

The book publishing world is also feeling the effects of this trend. As publishing houses merge due to economic pressures, many unique voices are left unheard. Publishers often focus on books that are guaranteed to sell right away, sidelining manuscripts that offer fresh ideas or challenge traditional narratives. Readers miss out on the richness that comes from diverse storytelling, as the market fills up with formulaic plots and clichés that prioritize profit over creativity.

As we think about the broader impacts of media consolidation, it's crucial to understand how our choices as consumers play a role in this cycle. In a world that increasingly values convenience, many people find themselves drawn to the most accessible content, often overlooking alternative stories that could offer new insights and experiences. The ease of getting content from a single source can unintentionally strengthen the concentration of cultural power, as viewers and readers ignore the many diverse options that exist beyond the mainstream.

Breaking this cycle of consumption is essential if we want to nurture a vibrant cultural landscape. It requires effort from all of us—consumers, creators, and advocates—to actively seek out and support independent voices. Whether it's watching independent films, reading books by underrepresented authors, or attending local music events, there are countless ways to push back against the forces of centralization. By making a conscious choice to engage with diverse content, we contribute to an environment that values variety and creativity over sameness.

When we explore the rules and regulations around media ownership, we also need to think about how government policies can either help or hinder diversity. The Federal Communications Commission (FCC) has played a significant role in shaping media ownership regulations over the years. However, as consolidation has sped up, there have been increasing calls for policy changes that protect cultural diversity and uplift independent creators. Advocates argue that stricter rules on media mergers and more support for independent media initiatives are necessary to counteract the negative effects of concentration.

For example, pushing for policies that require companies to invest in independent content or that create tax benefits for supporting diverse media can help level the playing field. Additionally, advocating for public funding for the arts and independent media outlets can give vital support to creators who might otherwise struggle in a competitive industry. By pushing for policies that prioritize cultural diversity, we can work toward a media landscape that encourages creativity and innovation instead of stifling them.

The future of our culture is at a crossroads. As we navigate this complex situation, we must be aware of the implications of media ownership concentration. It's crucial to advocate for a more fair media landscape where independent voices and diverse narratives can thrive. Our combined efforts can help shift the balance in favor of a richly varied cultural environment, where creativity flourishes, and all stories are given a chance to be told.

In this fight for cultural diversity, we must remember the power of our choices as consumers. By actively seeking out and supporting independent media, we can help create a more vibrant cultural ecosystem. The stories that shape our society should reflect the wide range of experiences within it. It's up to us to ensure that our cultural landscape remains diverse, innovative, and welcoming to all voices.

The time for change is now. We must recognize our role as active participants in shaping culture, challenging the norm, and pushing for a future that celebrates the richness of human expression. Through our collective actions, we can pave the way for a cultural revival that breathes new life into creativity and ensures that future generations inherit a landscape filled with diverse stories and experiences. The stakes are high, and the call for reform is urgent. Let's rise to the occasion and demand a media landscape that truly reflects the voices of our society, one that is inclusive and innovative.

Data-Driven Success

In today's world, where numbers and analytics reign supreme, streaming platforms have adopted a data-focused approach that dramatically changes how stories are created and shared. Algorithms have quietly become the main players—sometimes heroes, sometimes unseen troublemakers—shaping the entertainment scene. They offer guidance to producers and executives, helping them decide which stories are considered worthy of our time. But this leads to an important question: how does leaning on data impact the creativity that is the heart of storytelling?

At the center of the streaming revolution are powerful algorithms that can predict what viewers will like with surprising accuracy. These mathematical tools sift through mountains of viewer data, looking for behavior patterns that inform programming choices. Every time you play, pause, or rewind, these algorithms learn more about your tastes, crafting a personalized viewing experience just for you. At first, this may seem fantastic—who wouldn't want recommendations tailored to their preferences? But the implications of such precision are both wide-ranging and complicated.

Take, for example, a show that rises to fame largely because of its algorithmic appeal. Look at "Stranger Things," which has become a hallmark for Netflix. It hits many nostalgic notes: it evokes 1980s culture, taps into the fascination with supernatural themes, and pairs a family-friendly vibe with thrilling storylines. The show's success is clear, but it prompts a nagging question about originality. Was "Stranger Things" born from genuine creative spark, or was it carefully designed in response to data analysis?

This isn't to say that "Stranger Things" lacks creativity; rather, it's a reflection of a trend where analytics start to dictate creative choices. In the race to attract viewers, producers often lean heavily on familiar themes and formulas that have worked before. This can lead to a slew of shows that feel all too similar, each just a slight variation on the previous one. The outcome? A streaming world filled with content that plays it safe, favoring comfort over innovation.

Consider the many medical dramas that fill our screens—many are simply rehashes of the same idea. Each new show is designed with a clear understanding of audience preferences: intricate characters, intense situations, and a sprinkle of romantic tension. These shows often find success thanks to their data-driven nature; their stories are crafted to resonate with viewers. However, the heavy reliance on formulas can stifle the emergence of truly groundbreaking content that dares to challenge the usual norms and push the boundaries.

As we examine this data-driven approach, we also need to think about the audience's psychology. The sheer power of algorithms can create a culture of fear among creators. When success is so closely tied to viewer satisfaction metrics, the drive to take risks fades. A creator's artistic dreams can become overshadowed by corporate pressures that prioritize profit over creativity. As one screenwriter put it, "It feels like we're caught in a loop. Every idea I pitch is scrutinized through data. It's hard not to feel like I'm being asked to deliver a product instead of sharing a story."

This ongoing tension between creative dreams and data-driven demands is evident. Many creators find themselves in a difficult spot, balancing the desire to innovate with the need to secure funding for their projects. Stories that could potentially break new ground are often set aside for ones that promise quick returns. This creates a cycle where creativity gets stifled in favor of predictable stories, robbing the cultural landscape of the richness that unique storytelling can provide.

To illustrate this further, let's consider a producer who has worked in both independent and corporate settings. She shared, "When you're making an indie film, there's space to explore and take risks. You can create something that truly reflects your vision. But in a corporate environment, everything revolves around the numbers. There's constant research on what viewers want, and as a result, the essence of storytelling gets lost." This viewpoint highlights the struggles faced by creators who wish to push limits yet feel constrained by the watchful eye of data.

While the immediate financial perks of a data-driven strategy can be tempting, we need to think about the long-term effects. A culture that favors established formulas can lead to stagnation, where daring narratives find it hard to get a foothold. The rich variety of human experiences is boiled down into easily digestible segments, neatly fitting into the boxes defined by analytics. Consequently, the cultural scene becomes more homogeneous, often reflecting the interests of a few rather than the rich diversity of many.

Moreover, this trend affects us beyond the screen. When content turns formulaic, it shapes the very stories we consume and take to heart. Society's collective mindset may start to lean towards sameness, where fresh ideas are drowned out by a flood of remakes, sequels, and reboots. Audiences might unknowingly develop a taste for the familiar, fostering a cultural landscape that becomes increasingly resistant to change.

In discussions about this topic, many industry professionals voice their concerns for the future. There is a genuine worry that as long as data dictates decisions, the arts may be at risk. A seasoned director reflected, "The beauty of storytelling lies in its unpredictability. We need to take chances and explore the unknown. But when everything is calculated, that magic fades." This feeling echoes a broader desire for a return to the artistic exploration that characterizes the best of creative work.

So, how can we find a way to balance the powerful influence of data with the need for artistic risk-taking? One possible solution is to strike a balance that includes insights from data without letting them entirely control the creative process. Streaming platforms could look into hybrid models that encourage experimentation while still offering the benefits of analytics. This might involve investing in diverse storytelling projects or creating grants for unique ideas that might not have immediate commercial success.

Additionally, fostering collaboration between creators and data analysts could lead to exciting outcomes. When both groups work hand in hand, the potential for innovation could grow significantly. By honoring the art of storytelling while also using the insights provided by data, we could cultivate a more lively cultural scene that celebrates creativity.

Fortunately, some creators are already challenging the status quo. There are movements within the industry pushing for diverse voices and narratives that go against mainstream trends. Independent films and shows are gradually gaining recognition, showing that audiences truly crave authenticity. The success of projects like "The Farewell," which tells a personal story rooted in Chinese-American culture, illustrates the power of storytelling that breaks free from algorithmic constraints.

As viewers, we also play a significant role in shaping the cultural landscape. The choices we make about what to watch and support can influence the kinds of stories that continue to be told. By actively seeking out independent films, uplifting underrepresented voices, and advocating for diverse storytelling, we contribute to a cultural renaissance that values creativity over conformity. Our engagement can signal to platforms that there is indeed a market for innovation and willingness to take risks.

In navigating this intricate relationship between data and creativity, it's vital to stay optimistic. There is a strong desire for varied narratives that truly reflect the richness of human experiences. By recognizing the limitations of a purely data-driven approach, we can advocate for a cultural environment that encourages both artistic exploration and audience involvement.

The future of storytelling depends on our shared willingness to embrace risk, celebrate the unconventional, and support the diverse voices that enrich our cultural scene. This call to action is not just a plea for variety in media; it's an invitation to engage thoughtfully with the content we consume and to champion the art of storytelling in all its forms.

As we ponder the consequences of the data-driven approach, it becomes clear that we stand at a crucial crossroads. The world of content production is undergoing a transformation, and with that change comes a chance to reclaim the heart of storytelling. By nurturing an environment that values creativity alongside data analysis, we can pave the way for a cultural renaissance that honors the richness of diverse narratives.

The evolution of entertainment shouldn't merely be about the numbers; it should also be about the stories that connect with our hearts and minds. By fostering creativity, supporting innovative works, and advocating for a balanced blend of data and artistic expression, we can ensure that the stories we tell truly reflect the vibrant array of human experiences. This isn't just a battle for a better entertainment industry; it's a quest for cultural vitality that celebrates the many voices waiting to be heard.

Chapter 8: Nostalgia Sells: The Business of Stuck Culture

In today's world of consumerism, nostalgia has become a strong influence on what people buy and how brands market themselves. The saying "if it ain't broke, don't fix it" perfectly captures the mindset in many corporate boardrooms, where looking back to the past feels safe and familiar. Companies have figured out that tapping into warm, cherished memories can lead to big financial gains, creating a cycle of nostalgia-driven marketing that satisfies what consumers want while boosting company profits.

Nostalgia is more than just a sentimental longing for the past; it has turned into a smart marketing tactic that many businesses are using successfully. This strategy tends to work especially well during uncertain times, providing a comforting reminder of the simpler, happier days gone by. The emotional connections that people have with their past experiences can be powerful motivators and often lead to spur-of-the-moment buying. This isn't just sentimental fluff; it's a carefully thought-out approach that makes good financial sense. Companies know that nostalgia can generate better returns than trying to create totally new content, which often comes with more risk.

Let's look at a classic case in point—
Disney. The entertainment giant has mastered
the art of bringing back beloved franchises from
the past. Think about the remakes of animated
classics like "The Lion King" or "Aladdin."
These films aren't just retellings; they spark
nostalgia for older audiences while introducing
younger viewers to the magic of these stories.
The financial success of these remakes is
nothing short of staggering, raking in billions at
the box office worldwide. It's no surprise that
Disney heavily relies on nostalgia as they tap
into their vast library of beloved characters and
stories. By updating these tales with modern
visuals and technology, they create a strong
emotional connection that bridges generations.

This trend isn't limited to movies and
TV shows; it stretches into fashion, food, and
even technology. Vintage clothing has become a
popular choice for many people, with thrift
stores and boutiques thriving as shoppers
search for pieces that remind them of different
eras. Fast food chains have brought back classic
menu items to enthusiastic responses, tapping
into shared memories of taste and experience.
The rising popularity of retro tech, from vinyl
records to Polaroid cameras, shows a desire for
simpler times, often with a higher price tag.
Each of these trends highlights how nostalgia is
more than just a fleeting feeling; it's turning into
a real economic powerhouse.

However, like any strategy, using nostalgia has its risks and limits. Leaning too much on past successes can lead to a lack of creativity, where innovation takes a backseat to the comforting familiarity of what's already been done. Consumers might grow tired of the endless cycle of reboots and remakes, which could lead to a backlash against brands that seem devoid of fresh ideas. The saying "you can't go home again" rings true here; there's a point where nostalgia can actually work against you. If the market becomes flooded with remade content, it can lose its charm, making consumers question how genuine and original the offerings really are.

Additionally, there's a risk of alienating younger consumers who may not feel the same emotional connection to the past as older generations do. This disconnect can leave brands struggling to win over a group that craves newness rather than repetition. The challenge is to find that sweet spot between honoring the past and introducing something novel. Brands that can successfully combine nostalgia with fresh ideas will be in a better position to shine in a marketplace that is always changing.

There's plenty of data backing this trend. Market research firms are increasingly focusing on how consumers feel and behave in relation to nostalgic content. Studies show that nostalgia-based marketing can lead to stronger customer loyalty, increased spending, and even a willingness to pay higher prices. People are ready to spend their hard-earned money on products that bring back cherished memories or take them back to "the good old days." But this raises a question: how long can this approach last before the excitement fades and consumers crave something brand new?

The cyclical nature of nostalgia-driven products can also lead to market oversaturation. When the same franchises are constantly recycled, the initial excitement can quickly turn into boredom. A great example is the superhero genre; after years of dominating the box office, many viewers have expressed their weariness with what feels like an endless stream of superhero films. What used to be exciting reboots and spin-offs can start to feel tedious, resulting in lower box office returns and prompting studios to rethink their strategies.

We should also consider the possibility of cultural gatekeeping, where reviving certain nostalgic elements can push aside voices and stories that don't fit the mainstream narrative. Focusing too much on familiar franchises can overshadow opportunities for new creators and innovative ideas to emerge. This situation has consequences not only for the entertainment industry but also for society as a whole, as it encourages a cycle that favors the familiar over the groundbreaking.

However, nostalgia doesn't have to stifle creativity; it can actually spark it. By understanding the emotional ties that consumers have to the past, brands can use these feelings to create new narratives and foster innovative partnerships. For instance, a company might take an iconic character and place them in a new setting or story, paying tribute to the past while also introducing fresh ideas. This requires skill and a good grasp of market trends, but it is definitely possible.

Ultimately, nostalgia is a double-edged sword. It can drive sales and create strong bonds with consumers, but it can also lead to stagnation and boredom if not handled carefully. As businesses navigate this complex landscape, they need to weigh the immediate benefits of nostalgia-driven strategies against the long-term effects on cultural innovation. The real challenge is to embrace the past while nurturing fresh ideas, ensuring that the future stays vibrant and full of potential.

As we observe the ongoing changes in consumer culture, one thing is certain: nostalgia will continue to play a significant role in shaping the marketplace. What remains to be seen is whether it will be a force for growth or a limitation on creativity. In the end, the answer lies in the hands of consumers, who both hold onto the past and look forward to what's next.

Intellectual Property Trends

In a world that loves looking back, the rules around intellectual property law are becoming a crucial part of how we express ourselves creatively. These laws do more than just protect the rights of creators; they can trap beloved characters and stories in complicated legal struggles, resulting in a never-ending stream of reboots and remakes. Intellectual property is designed to encourage new ideas by protecting the hard work of creators. However, what happens when these protections turn into ways for companies to monopolize creative content, making it harder for fresh voices and ideas to shine?

To understand the impact of intellectual property trends, we first need to look at why they are used in the first place. In the entertainment world—especially film, TV, and gaming—companies have become experts in tapping into nostalgia, using the strong emotional ties people have to their favorite franchises. Take the Marvel Cinematic Universe, for instance. It hasn't just taken over the box office; it has built a complex network of stories based on years of comic book history. This situation is more than about storytelling; it's also about ownership. Marvel's extensive collection of characters, all carefully protected by intellectual property laws, allows them to easily recycle and adapt content, while pulling in huge profits.

But the appeal of these established franchises goes beyond just marketing; it's a smart business strategy, too. Companies can pour a lot of resources into developing new stories and characters, but the risk of failing looms large. On the other hand, bringing back a beloved character or story carries much less risk, tapping into audience nostalgia and often ensuring a better return on investment. This cycle of relying on nostalgic franchises leads to a situation where companies focus more on what's already popular, often at the expense of original storytelling. While this approach may bring quick profits, it stifles long-term creativity, leaving little room for new ideas to grow.

Yet, the trend of reboots and remakes carries its own set of challenges. The idea of "franchise fatigue" is popping up as audiences start to get bored with the constant flow of familiar characters and predictable plots. While nostalgia can kick off excitement, it can quickly turn into indifference when consumers realize they're being served the same content over and over again. Recent pushbacks against certain film franchises highlight this fatigue; viewers are eager for something new, a call for fresh creativity in a landscape filled with familiar comfort.

This brings us to an important question: who really controls the narrative? The massive influence wielded by a few corporations over cultural stories raises concerns. As intellectual property laws tightly enforce ownership, companies can effectively gatekeep which stories get the spotlight. This can lead to a cultural blend where new talent struggles to break through, and diverse perspectives often get pushed to the edges. This monopolization of intellectual property creates barriers for emerging creators, making it harder for them to find their footing in a market already overflowing with remakes.

The consequences for new creators are significant. When big players dominate the scene, the chances for innovation shrink, and the voices of fresh talent risk being lost in the shuffle. New creators might find themselves in a tough spot: they want to explore new narratives and tell unique stories, but the frameworks of intellectual property law can stifle their creativity. With established franchises taking up most of the space, they often have to navigate a system that favors familiarity over originality.

For example, the gaming industry illustrates the struggles posed by this landscape. Just look at the many remasters and remakes of classic games that have come out in recent years. While nostalgia can drive initial sales, one has to wonder: is this really the best use of creative talent? Developers may feel pushed into reviving old games rather than exploring new ideas. This overwhelming focus on past content can lead to a standstill in creativity, where innovation takes a backseat to the lure of easy profits.

The cycle of reboots and remakes creates a feedback loop that can stifle cultural growth. By constantly recycling past hits, the industry risks missing out on the chance to explore new themes, voices, and stories that could resonate with today's audiences. At its core, the preservation of cultural narratives should not come at the cost of creativity and expression.

As audiences grow more aware of these trends, there's a rising demand for originality. People are tired of the same content dressed up in new packaging. They crave fresh ideas, innovative storytelling, and diverse narratives that reflect the rich complexities of modern life. This shift in expectations from consumers presents a challenge for companies as they try to find the right balance between riding the nostalgia wave and nurturing new ideas.

The debate around intellectual property isn't limited to entertainment. Similar patterns can be seen in areas like fashion and literature. Fashion brands often bring back old styles, while authors might revisit classic themes, resulting in a market that feels more like a recycling bin than a vibrant creative space. When creativity becomes just a game of rebranding, the cultural fabric can start to fray.

Yet, there is a silver lining. The dialogue around intellectual property is changing, opening the door for new possibilities. Emerging creators are taking advantage of social media and online platforms to share their stories and connect with audiences directly. By breaking through traditional barriers, they can carve out their own niche in a crowded market. This shift toward democratizing creativity challenges the norm and fosters innovation, injecting new life into an industry bogged down by nostalgia.

As the landscape of intellectual property continues to evolve, it's vital for consumers to stay engaged. Supporting original content, uplifting new voices, and asking for diversity in storytelling can help combat the effects of franchise fatigue. Audiences have the power to influence the narrative by choosing where they spend their money, encouraging companies to invest in fresh ideas instead of relying solely on the familiar.

The implications of these trends reach beyond entertainment; they touch on the essence of cultural evolution. As society navigates rapid technological changes and shifting values, the stories we tell and the narratives we prioritize will play a vital role in shaping our future. By valuing creativity and supporting new talent, we can create an environment where innovation thrives, leading to a lively and dynamic cultural landscape.

Ultimately, the rules around intellectual property law are more than just regulations about ownership; they reflect our shared values and priorities. As we navigate this complex landscape, it's increasingly important to advocate for a culture that embraces both nostalgia and originality. By understanding the power dynamics at play and pushing for change, we can build a future where creativity flourishes and the voices of all creators are heard. The challenge lies in balancing the pull of the past with the promise of what's still to come, ensuring that the stories we choose to tell reflect the rich diversity of human experience.

Emotional Appeal

Nostalgia—a word that brings to mind simpler times and treasured memories—holds a special place in our emotional lives. It calls to us like a gentle reminder, inviting us to reflect on the past. But part of what makes nostalgia so captivating is what it isn't; it's not just a yearning for the good old days or a naive belief that everything was better back then. Instead, nostalgia is a rich emotional experience that mixes comfort with longing, blending both warmth and sadness into one complex feeling. It acts like a soothing balm for our busy lives, allowing us a moment to escape into a world that once felt safer and more predictable.

Psychologically, we can think of nostalgia as a sentimental longing for the past, often accompanied by a deep desire for things that are, or may always be, out of reach. This feeling can be sparked by many things—like a song, a familiar scent, or even an old photograph. Yet, its impact goes beyond just ourselves; it shapes our shared experiences and cultural stories. For example, remember the last time a classic song played on the radio, instantly whisking you back to carefree summer days or key moments in your life? That's the power of nostalgia; it's not just something we experience alone; it's something that bonds us through shared memories.

Brands have picked up on this powerful emotion and use it to connect with consumers. A look at successful advertising campaigns shows a clear trend: tapping into the feelings of the past can forge strong bonds with customers, leading to lasting loyalty. Take Coca-Cola, for instance. Their nostalgic marketing, featuring their iconic polar bears, retro advertisements, and classic glass bottles, whisks us away to a time filled with warmth and tradition. When you enjoy a Coke, it's not merely about quenching your thirst; it's about reliving memories of family gatherings, summer barbecues, and joyful celebrations. Coca-Cola creates not just a product, but an experience that evokes feelings of safety and familiarity, making it more than just a drink.

The revival of vinyl records showcases the influence of nostalgia on how we consume. In a world dominated by digital music, the hands-on experience of placing a needle on a record, combined with the rich, warm sound, gives many a sense of authenticity that feels lacking in today's fast-paced, tech-driven lives. The return of vinyl isn't just a trend; it's a collective desire to reconnect with the past, to embrace a more analog experience in a digital world. For many, buying a vinyl record is not just about music; it's an emotional journey back to the sounds and culture of their youth. It's a cherished ritual, offering an escape from the relentless pace of modern life.

However, as we lean into these nostalgic feelings, we must ask ourselves: What might we lose in our search for comfort? When we cling to the familiar, we might unintentionally dampen innovation and creativity. Nostalgia can be a double-edged sword; while it feels nice to revisit beloved characters and stories, getting too comfortable in the past may dull our enthusiasm for the present and future. By seeking comfort in what we already know, we might miss out on the exciting possibilities that lie ahead, putting cultural evolution at risk.

Nostalgia doesn't just affect us as individuals; it also plays a big role in how we form collective memories and cultural identities. Consider how certain movies, songs, or fashion trends become symbols of specific times. They act as cultural anchors, connecting us through shared experiences. During tough times or uncertainty, people often seek comfort in familiar things, bonding over the collective memory of what once was. This can create a sense of community, where we come together to reminisce and celebrate shared moments. But it can also lead to a simplified view of history, overlooking the complexities and challenges that shaped those times.

The effects of nostalgia are both profound and sometimes contradictory. On one hand, it creates a sense of belonging and connection, helping us bond over shared memories. On the other hand, it can lead to an idealized view of the past, glossing over the difficulties that come with any era. This mixed nature of nostalgia can lead to a longing that's more about escaping reality than truly reflecting on it. While it can strengthen our sense of identity, depending too much on nostalgia can stall cultural growth and exploration of new stories.

Instead of being merely a comforting place to retreat, nostalgia can shape our cultural preferences. As audiences watch films and enjoy media that looks back to the past, they might start to favor familiarity over new ideas, reinforcing the trend of reboots and remakes. The real danger here is cultural complacency; when we continuously reach into the past, we risk stifling innovation. This raises an important question: How can we honor what has come before while also embracing the opportunities that the present and future hold? How do we find a balance that allows us to respect the past while still welcoming new ideas?

Striking this balance is not just an abstract idea; it's something that creators and consumers should actively ponder. Both individuals and companies can bring fresh ideas into familiar stories. By reimagining beloved narratives, creators can breathe new life into old tales, honoring what we love while also paving the way for new stories to unfold. This back-and-forth between past and present can lead to a more vibrant cultural conversation, encouraging both reflection and innovation.

Equally important is what we, as consumers, can do. By supporting originality and seeking out diverse narratives, we can challenge what's familiar and uplift new voices. This isn't just about personal taste; it's a call to action. Choosing to engage with fresh ideas can spark a broader cultural shift, where innovation is celebrated, not just tolerated. As consumers, we have the power to influence which stories thrive and which are left behind.

The emotional pull of nostalgia is a complex force, bringing both advantages and challenges. While it can create a sense of connection and belonging, relying too heavily on nostalgia can hinder creativity and progress. As we navigate the maze of cultural change, it's essential to consider what we choose to celebrate and remember. Are we truly honoring the past, or are we allowing it to trap us in a cycle where we just repeat what's come before? By embracing both nostalgia and originality, we can build a richer, more diverse cultural landscape that celebrates our shared memories and the exciting possibilities that lie ahead.

In this ongoing discussion about nostalgia and its emotional charm, we're left to think about how we can nurture a culture that appreciates both the comfort of what we know and the eagerness for what's new. The challenge rests not only in the stories we tell but in the choices we make as consumers and creators. As we explore our emotional ties to the past, let's stay mindful of nostalgia's allure, ensuring it serves as a bridge to new adventures rather than a barrier to fresh ideas.

Chapter 9: Microcultures on the Fringe: Is There Still Hope for Innovation?

In today's world, it can often feel like innovation is just a memory, a bright flame that has dimmed over time. But even in the shadows of stagnation, small fires of creativity and originality are still burning, sparking the imaginations of those brave enough to explore the edges of society. These microcultures, which often go unnoticed by the mainstream, serve as rich soil for innovative ideas, helping them grow and evolve in surprising and inspiring ways.

Think of microcultures as hidden treasures, tucked away in the corners of our society, waiting for someone to discover them. They thrive outside the usual boundaries, driven by passionate groups of people who refuse to blend in. Whether it's a vibrant art community in an old warehouse, an underground music scene, or a local movement fighting for social change, these microcultures challenge the status quo and act as springboards for fresh ideas.

A great example can be found in the realm of independent music. Many artists now operate beyond the reach of record labels and mainstream radio. Take the rise of bedroom pop, a genre that has exploded in popularity thanks to platforms like SoundCloud and

Bandcamp. Musicians like Clairo and Rex Orange County gained attention through DIY recordings shared online, breaking away from traditional paths to fame. This wave of creativity is marked by its lo-fi sound and personal lyrics, capturing the raw and authentic experiences of today's youth.

What really makes these microcultures powerful is their ability to foster innovation through community. In the bedroom pop scene, creators often work together, share resources, and support each other in ways that larger companies simply can't match. This sense of togetherness creates an environment where experimentation can flourish, leading to new sounds, styles, and ways of expressing art. The result is a lively community buzzing with creativity, where the only limits on innovation are the imaginations of those involved.

Fashion, too, is filled with exciting microcultures that push against mainstream trends. Consider the growing movement of upcycling, where people take old clothes and turn them into brand-new, unique pieces. This trend has become popular among those who care about the environment and want to reject fast fashion's wasteful cycle, choosing instead to express themselves through personal, sustainable fashion. Small brands and individual creators are at the forefront of this movement, often making statements about consumerism while showcasing their artistic skills.

There's a special energy that radiates from these niche communities. The people involved are often driven by a sense of purpose, wanting to create something meaningful that resonates with their values and beliefs. This passion spreads like wildfire, encouraging others to take risks and explore their own creative journeys. As these microcultures continue to grow, they remind us that innovation doesn't always come from the top. Sometimes, it blossoms from the ground up.

One striking example of this is in the world of visual arts. Street art, once pushed to the sidelines, has become a powerful form of expression that challenges societal norms. Artists like Banksy and Shepard Fairey are famous worldwide, but it's the many unknown street artists who truly capture the spirit of innovation. Armed with spray paint and a message, they turn urban spaces into canvases, speaking out against injustice and sparking conversations about important issues. These street art microcultures unite diverse voices, reflecting the complexities of the communities they come from.

The internet has been a game-changer for these microcultures, too. With platforms like Instagram, TikTok, and Reddit, creators can showcase their work, connect with others who share their interests, and build communities around their passions. This shift in creativity has allowed niche interests to thrive, creating spaces where new ideas are celebrated instead of stifled. From DIY home improvement fans sharing their projects on YouTube to fan fiction writers crafting intricate worlds based on their favorite movies, the opportunities for collaboration and experimentation are truly endless.

What's exciting about microcultures is not only their ability to generate innovative ideas but also their power to influence larger cultural movements. When these small communities gain traction, they can disrupt mainstream narratives and bring about change in unexpected ways. For example, the rise of veganism can be traced back to grassroots movements that promoted plant-based living as a lifestyle choice steeped in ethics and sustainability. As more people embraced this way of life, it crossed over into the mainstream, prompting major food brands to offer more vegan-friendly options.

Similarly, the renewed interest in analog formats like vinyl records, film photography, and cassette tapes can be linked to microcultures that celebrate nostalgia while resisting today's digital overload. Record stores have transformed into community hubs where enthusiasts gather to share their love for music, often discovering new artists and genres in the process. This movement highlights the joy of experiencing music and photography in a tangible way, encouraging us to slow down in an increasingly fast-paced world.

Even though the dominant cultural narrative might often seem stagnant, these innovative sparks remind us that creativity is vibrant and alive in the microcultures on the edges of society. They invite us to reconnect with our own passions, to find the extraordinary in the everyday, and to follow the unconventional paths that lead to groundbreaking ideas. By supporting these communities and acknowledging their contributions, we can create an environment that nurtures innovation in all its exciting forms, helping us break free from the cultural freeze that has held us back for too long.

As we explore these microcultures, we're reminded that innovation isn't just for the elite or the well-connected; it's something anyone can tap into. It's a living, breathing phenomenon that thrives in the hands of those who dare to think outside the box. By shining a light on these pockets of creativity and celebrating their resourcefulness, we can reignite the flames of innovation that have flickered in recent years, setting the stage for a lively cultural renaissance. Each spark, each idea, and each individual helps weave a larger narrative filled with promise and potential.

Ultimately, the key to our innovative future lies in recognizing and supporting the small communities that are making waves, often in the background. These microcultures hold the possibility of a brighter cultural landscape, one that values creativity, teamwork, and the boldness to embrace what's different. In a world that sometimes seems to push against original thought, let's take inspiration from those who continue to push boundaries, challenge norms, and ignite the innovative sparks that light our way forward.

Niche Communities

In the vastness of the online world, where mainstream culture often takes the spotlight, niche communities sparkle like hidden treasures waiting to be discovered. These groups, often found in places like Discord servers, Telegram chats, and niche subreddits, create their own unique cultures that celebrate specific interests and passions. They break away from the usual trends, offering a vibrant space where individuals connect, collaborate, and unleash their creativity. Here, people can express themselves freely, away from the limitations of conventional norms.

Picture a lively online space buzzing with excitement, where individuals who might feel alone or out of place in their daily lives discover a true sense of belonging. That's the magic of niche communities—they connect people across distances, uniting them over shared interests that often get overlooked in wider society. Whether it's a passion for a particular music genre, an unusual hobby, or an obscure TV show, these communities form deep bonds that can change lives in meaningful ways.

The interactions within these groups are truly captivating. They thrive on collaboration, support, and celebrating each person's unique creativity. Unlike larger platforms, where popular content typically gets all the attention thanks to algorithms, niche communities cherish authenticity and originality. Members dive into discussions, share their creations, and provide feedback, creating an environment where experimentation is encouraged. It's a safe haven where individuals can take creative risks without the pressure to achieve commercial success.

Take fan art communities, for instance. Artists bring their favorite characters and stories to life in fresh ways. Websites like DeviantArt or Tumblr have become hotspots for these creative souls. In these spaces, art transforms into a conversation—a way for fans to express their love while also critiquing what they adore. Artists often thrive in this environment, pushing their creative limits and exploring new techniques, styles, and stories. The collaborative spirit encourages sharing knowledge and resources, as experienced artists guide newcomers, celebrating each other's achievements along the way.

This sense of cooperation spreads beyond just art. Many niche communities focus on specific skills or interests, such as the flourishing DIY movement. People share tutorials, give advice, and showcase their projects, creating a treasure trove of knowledge that opens up creativity to everyone. In these spaces, the barriers to learning new crafts or hobbies are lowered, and anyone eager to get started can find a wealth of resources within reach. The joy of making something with your own hands is magnified by the support of a community that genuinely appreciates each member's contributions.

However, while these communities nurture creativity, they aren't without their challenges. The very nature of niche culture can sometimes lead to a lack of diversity in ideas, turning these groups into echo chambers. Within these spaces, fresh ideas can stall, and differing opinions may be silenced. This trend is especially noticeable in online environments, where algorithms steer content based on what users like, further locking individuals into their echo chambers. When everyone shares similar beliefs or tastes, the chances of losing touch with the wider cultural conversation grow.

Take conspiracy theory communities, for example. What might start as a niche interest fueled by a quest for alternative perspectives can evolve into insular groups that spread misinformation. The connections formed in these communities can become so strong that questioning shared beliefs can lead to exclusion. This kind of insularity can be especially risky in an age where the lines between fact and fiction can easily blur, sometimes leading to serious consequences.

Despite these potential issues, we can't overlook the positive impacts of niche communities. These spaces often give rise to new forms of expression and innovative ideas that challenge the usual way of thinking. The overlap between niche communities and larger cultural movements highlights their importance in the creative world. They often serve as breeding grounds for subcultures that, with time, can gain momentum and influence broader societal changes.

Take the "cottagecore" aesthetic, for instance. This movement, which romanticizes rural life, simplicity, and sustainability, started in niche online communities where people shared their love for homesteading, traditional crafts, and a slower lifestyle. As this movement grew, it spilled over into mainstream culture, affecting fashion, home decor, and even how we view our connection with nature. Thanks to social media, the cottagecore movement has ignited discussions about sustainability and self-sufficiency that reach far beyond its original circles.

The gaming world also offers a fascinating perspective on the power of niche communities. Online gaming has blossomed into vibrant hubs of culture, where players unite to share experiences, strategies, and fan-made content. Games like "Animal Crossing" and "Stardew Valley" have sparked communities centered on cooperation, creativity, and social interaction. Players share tips for crafting beautiful in-game spaces, showcase their dream addresses, and even collaborate on ambitious projects that enhance the gaming experience beyond just the screen. The friendships formed in these communities often lead to lasting connections and collaborations that enrich the gaming journey.

As we take a closer look at these niche communities, it's clear they hold a vital place in our broader cultural landscape. They act as testing grounds for fresh ideas and expressions, often providing a counter-narrative to mainstream culture. Their significance lies in how they challenge the norm and inspire people to look at things in new ways.

The diversity found in niche communities highlights our human capacity for creativity and connection. From vintage video games to unique discussions about lesser-known literary genres, these microcultures showcase the richness of human experience. They remind us that innovation doesn't always come from universities or corporate offices; sometimes, it blooms in the most unexpected corners of society.

Moreover, the links between these niche communities and larger cultural movements deepen our understanding of what innovation truly means. Each small community adds to the larger creative narrative, weaving a complex web of influence that can significantly shift the cultural landscape. For instance, social media has enabled niche communities to thrive and profoundly impact mainstream culture. Trends that start in these small circles often find their way into popular culture, proving the fluidity and excitement of cultural exchange.

In celebrating these niche communities, we also recognize the importance of balance. It's crucial to foster inclusivity while keeping the essence of these spaces intact. Encouraging diverse voices within niche communities can help avoid the risks of becoming too insular or stagnant. When people with different perspectives come together, the potential for innovation grows significantly. The richness of ideas that arise from such collaborations can lead to groundbreaking expressions that challenge existing norms and push boundaries.

While it may be easy to brush off niche communities as just online subcultures, their influence on the wider cultural landscape is undeniable. They serve as nurturing grounds for creativity, allowing individuals the freedom to explore their passions without the constraints of mainstream pressures. These communities provide an escape from conformity and commercialism, making room for genuine expression and the pursuit of new ideas.

As we navigate this intricate cultural landscape, embracing the uniqueness of niche communities becomes essential. They hold the keys to innovation, creativity, and expression that go beyond fleeting trends. By supporting and engaging with these microcultures, we celebrate the diversity of human experience, encourage collaboration, and fan the flames of creativity that quietly flicker in the shadows. In a world that often favors louder voices, it is within the whispers of niche communities that we may uncover the most profound insights and inspirations—reminding us that hope for innovation can always be found, even on the fringes.

Catalysts for Change

Change in culture doesn't just appear out of nowhere, like Athena springing from

Zeus's head. Instead, it often simmers quietly beneath the surface, sparked by small, local movements that may seem unimportant at first. The magic of microcultures lies in their ability to nurture ideas and creativity that can ripple out and create waves of change in the wider cultural scene. These unique communities, with their fresh viewpoints and practices, can challenge the norm, pushing us to rethink how we engage with and appreciate culture around us.

To grasp how these microcultures can drive change, we need to consider visibility. How can we make sure that the inventive ideas coming from these small, often overlooked communities arc recognized and appreciated in the broader cultural conversation? This is a vital question. Without visibility, even the most groundbreaking ideas can stay stifled, hidden away in the shadows of mainstream culture.

History offers us many examples of grassroots movements making a real impact on mainstream culture. Take the punk rock movement of the late 1970s and early 1980s, for instance. Born from the underground music scene, punk didn't just give us a new genre of music; it ignited a revolution in fashion, art, and social attitudes. Embracing a do-it-yourself spirit, punk rejected corporate control and commercialism, leading to a wave of independent record labels and a fierce commitment to being authentic. The energy and defiance of punk changed countless artists and influenced subcultures, leaving a mark on today's cultural landscape.

Similarly, the LGBTQ+ rights movement began as a reaction to oppression and discrimination and has reshaped societal views on gender and sexual identity. Through grassroots activism, pride parades, and the visibility of queer artists, this movement has not just paved the way for greater acceptance; it has inspired a wealth of cultural expressions. From the lively drag scene to queer literature that challenges traditional narratives, the impact is deep and far-reaching.

In recent years, we've seen the rise of various microcultures, often thanks to social media. These online spaces create a welcoming environment for niche communities to grow. For instance, the "Black Lives Matter" movement started from grassroots activism and has gained momentum on platforms like Twitter and Instagram, turning a local struggle into a worldwide conversation. The visibility that social media provides has propelled issues of racial justice to the forefront of cultural discussions across the globe.

While we celebrate these successes, it's also important to look closely at the challenges these movements face. One major issue is corporate co-optation. When a grassroots idea starts to gain traction, it often catches the eye of big companies looking to profit from its popularity. What started as a movement rooted in authenticity can quickly become commercialized, losing its original meaning. A clear example of this can be seen in the fashion industry's appropriation of streetwear. Originally a product of urban culture, streetwear has been embraced by high fashion brands, creating an uneasy mix of authenticity and profit. Although this can bring the style into the mainstream, the heart of its origin often gets lost along the way.

Furthermore, mainstream media tends to overlook voices from non-conformist communities in favor of stories that fit neatly into established narratives. This bias can stifle diversity and limit how fringe communities are represented. Media outlets often focus on sensational stories, favoring conflict over the rich, nuanced discussions that microcultures encourage. This focus can paint a distorted picture of these communities, reinforcing stereotypes and downplaying their contributions to larger cultural dialogues.

When we think about cultural trends, it's important to consider their cyclical nature. Cultural cycles often reflect the rise and fall of trends; what was once out of style can come back, often with a new twist. This cycle creates a fertile ground for microcultures to thrive, as they can offer fresh perspectives that challenge mainstream ideas. For example, the comeback of vintage fashion shows how a desire for authenticity and sustainability has sparked interest in thrift shopping and upcycling. What began as a niche movement has had a significant effect on our view of fashion, leading to a more thoughtful approach to consumption.

Embracing the innovations that come from these microcultures is crucial. It calls for us to be open-minded, to listen to voices that differ from our own, and to celebrate diversity. Supporting underground movements means actively seeking out and amplifying their contributions, whether through social media, independent publications, or community events.

Think about the influence of local art scenes, which often highlight the work of emerging artists who may not yet have a place in mainstream galleries. By attending shows in alternative spaces, sharing their work online, and building a supportive community, we create an environment where creativity can thrive. This not only helps the artists but also enriches our entire cultural landscape.

We should also recognize the connections between the innovations from fringe cultures and the larger conversations shaping our world. The rise of mental health awareness, for instance, is often linked to grassroots movements advocating for greater understanding and acceptance. Social media campaigns, self-help initiatives, and support groups have all contributed to changing how we view mental health. This shift has opened up broader cultural discussions that challenge stigmas and promote vulnerability, helping us build a more compassionate society.

Encouraging engagement with these innovative sparks can create a ripple effect that crosses cultural boundaries. Celebrating creativity in all its forms—whether through art, music, fashion, or activism—fuels a shared understanding that embraces diversity. It reminds us that progress isn't straightforward; it's a complex web of interactions shaped by microcultures that often challenge our preconceived ideas.

As we navigate the diverse landscape of culture, it's clear that microcultures are not just pockets of resistance; they are vibrant ecosystems holding the keys to our collective future. By embracing the creativity and innovation that springs from these communities, we foster an environment where diverse voices can shine and new ideas can thrive.

By supporting these movements, we cultivate a culture of inclusivity and appreciation for the many forms of expression that surround us. Each microculture adds to the larger story, weaving a rich narrative of human experience that challenges the ordinary and inspires the extraordinary.

Engaging with these underground movements means stepping outside our comfort zones. It encourages us to actively seek out voices and expressions that differ from our own, broadening our understanding of creativity and innovation. By doing this, we not only enhance our individual perspectives but also help create a cultural landscape that values diversity and encourages collaboration.

This exploration into the world of microcultures reminds us that change is within reach, ignited by the vibrant, creative expressions found on the fringes. We can become catalysts for change ourselves, championing the causes that resonate with us and supporting the movements that inspire us. Together, we can build a cultural ecosystem that honors the contributions of all, allowing innovation to thrive and guiding us toward a more inclusive and imaginative future.

In this constantly changing landscape, let's celebrate the small victories and quiet revolutions that happen within microcultures. They may not always make the news, but their effects can be deep. By nurturing these underground movements and amplifying their voices, we harness the power of creativity to shape a better tomorrow—one where diversity is cherished, innovation is celebrated, and cultural change is not just possible, but inevitable.

Marcus Lears

Chapter 10: Breaking Free: How We Can Escape Stuck Culture

Today, we're faced with more choices than ever before, and that's where the idea of conscious consumption shines through as a guiding light. It encourages us to think carefully about how we spend our money and the impact those choices have on our world. Instead of just grabbing whatever is on sale, we're invited to take an active role in shaping the culture around us. The way we buy things doesn't just affect our own lives; it sends ripples through society, influencing the economy and the creative spirit that we all want to see flourish.

At the heart of conscious consumption is the understanding of what our purchases mean. It's about looking at where our products come from, the stories they tell, and the values they represent. We should be asking ourselves important questions: What message are we supporting with our money? Are we opting for mass-produced items that lack character and artistry? Or are we seeking out local artisans and independent creators who prioritize sustainability and ethical practices? These decisions are significant, not only for our immediate happiness but for the larger impact they have on culture and innovation.

Consider fast fashion. It started as a smart way to offer trendy clothes at low prices, but it has turned into a massive industry driven by our desire for the latest styles. Unfortunately, this relentless demand comes with a heavy price for both our planet and the creativity in the fashion world. While fast fashion brands quickly produce disposable clothing that often lacks meaning, independent designers and smaller labels pour heart and soul into their work, crafting pieces with unique stories. By choosing to support these creators, we encourage a culture that values art and craftsmanship over mere consumption.

Moreover, embracing conscious consumption can help counteract the overwhelming influence of big corporations that often stifle creativity. These companies typically focus on profits, leading to a bland uniformity rather than diverse creativity. We see this in media, where blockbuster films and mainstream music dominate, leaving little room for new ideas. By seeking out independent films, underground music, and local art, we not only uplift alternative voices but also create demand for a richer variety of artistic expression. This way, we can slowly chip away at the hold that corporate interests have over our cultural experiences.

The shift toward being more conscious in our consumption habits is something that should be celebrated. It represents a collective awakening—a realization that supporting independent and innovative creators is a powerful way to resist cultural stagnation. When we invest in creativity, we help nurture a community centered around collaboration, conversation, and sharing different viewpoints. In a time when social media can often divide us, supporting local artists and creators can bring us together, forming connections that go beyond simple transactions.

This cultural change asks us to rethink what we value as consumers. The idea that we can vote with our wallets is more than just a saying; it holds real meaning. Every purchase reflects our priorities and beliefs. By choosing to support sustainable practices, ethical production, and innovative artistry, we tell the market that we want a different kind of cultural experience—one that is rich, lively, and truly representative of our diverse human stories.

Education plays a key role in building this culture of conscious consumption. We need to equip ourselves with knowledge about the products we buy, learning where they come from and how they affect the world. Media literacy is particularly vital in this digital age, where misinformation travels fast. Being able to critically analyze what we read and view is essential. By developing a discerning eye for the content we consume, we not only enrich our own experiences but also elevate the conversation around art and creativity.

There's also a tremendous opportunity beyond our personal choices to engage with creative projects that reflect our values. This could mean shopping at local farmers' markets, buying handmade items from independent artisans, or subscribing to independent media that challenge mainstream viewpoints. Each small action contributes to a broader movement toward a more lively and varied cultural landscape.

Additionally, practicing conscious consumption means navigating the digital world with intention. The rise of streaming services and social media has opened up access to a wealth of art and culture, allowing artists from all backgrounds to share their work. However, we must be careful of algorithms that can trap us in echo chambers, where we only see what aligns with our existing preferences. To break out of this bubble, we should actively look for diverse voices and stories, stepping outside our comfort zones to discover the richness in unfamiliar creative expressions.

Engaging in conscious consumption doesn't mean sacrificing enjoyment. In fact, it enhances our experiences. When our choices are rooted in intention and understanding, we grow to appreciate the art and culture around us on a deeper level. Attending a local theater performance becomes more than just a night out; it turns into a shared celebration of creativity and community. Similarly, enjoying a meal made from locally sourced ingredients transforms dinner into a meaningful connection with the land and those who cultivate it.

Even sharing our discoveries can help amplify this cultural shift. Recommendations from friends, social media posts that highlight independent creators, and community events featuring local art all contribute to raising awareness and excitement about conscious consumption. By supporting those who are bravely pushing the boundaries of creativity, we help maintain a culture that thrives on innovation and expression.

As we navigate this landscape of consumption, it's important to realize that conscious consumption isn't a one-size-fits-all approach. Each of us has different preferences, situations, and resources that will shape how we interact with this idea. Yet, the core principle is clear: being mindful of our consumption habits empowers us to influence our cultural environment, creating a space where creativity can thrive.

As we work together to break free from cultural stagnation, embracing conscious consumption offers a pathway to a brighter cultural future. It invites each of us to be more thoughtful participants in the cultural ecosystem. By aligning our values with the choices we make, we can build a society that celebrates innovation, supports a variety of artistic voices, and rekindles the creative spirit that once burned so brightly.

In the grand scheme of culture, our choices act like individual threads that come together to create a richer, more intricate picture. Every mindful decision we make adds to the cultural landscape we want to be part of. As we navigate the complexities of modern life, let's not forget that the power to create change lies not just in grand gestures but in the choices we make every day. By embracing conscious consumption, we can start to carve a new path forward—one that champions creativity, innovation, and the beautiful human spirit in all its forms.

Education and Media Literacy

In this age of information, we're surrounded by an incredible amount of content—exciting, refreshing, and sometimes just plain overwhelming. This flood of information can be both a blessing and a burden, offering us knowledge and connection while also risking our immersion in lies and cultural dullness. This is where education comes in, especially when it comes to media literacy. Understanding how culture works has never been more important if we want to break free from stagnation.

Cultural stagnation is that nagging feeling of unease that many of us sense but can't quite put into words. It often comes from not fully grasping the hidden forces that shape our media world. From big companies focusing on profit instead of creativity to nostalgia-driven stories that just recycle old ideas, several factors trap us in a cycle of sameness. Educating ourselves and others about these issues is vital. When we become aware of the patterns that influence our culture, we gain the power to look for new ideas and step away from the dullness that often defines stagnant cultures.

Think about how social media and streaming platforms use algorithms to decide what we see. Every day, users are hit with suggestions based on what they've liked before, which can create a bubble that limits our exposure to fresh ideas. This becomes even more concerning when we realize that these algorithms aren't neutral; they often highlight sensational and trending topics, sidelining meaningful discussions and innovative concepts. By adding media literacy to school curricula—from elementary classrooms to universities—we can arm students with the critical thinking skills they need for today's media landscape. They'll learn not just to question where their information comes from but also to engage with a wide range of cultural expressions, pushing back against the oversimplified stories and corporate spin that often dominate our media.

Promoting media literacy is absolutely crucial. In a world where misinformation spreads rapidly and "fake news" is part of our everyday chats, the ability to separate fact from fiction is a skill that should be nurtured from an early age. Imagine a classroom where students actively critique news articles, analyze ads, and discuss the implications of viral videos. This isn't just an academic exercise; it fosters a generation of informed consumers and creators who understand the importance of their engagement with media. Skills like recognizing biases, understanding persuasive techniques, and appreciating different perspectives will define educated individuals in the media landscape of tomorrow.

Aside from formal education, we also need to look at informal settings to promote critical thinking and media literacy. Workshops, discussion groups, and online forums can be great spaces for ideas to thrive, offering opportunities for people to come together and analyze cultural content. These environments encourage conversation and help untangle the complexities of the media world, allowing participants to express their concerns, share their thoughts, and learn from one another. It's in these exchanges that the seeds of cultural progress are planted, helping individuals feel empowered to question the norms and advocate for new narratives.

Education also plays a vital role in fueling activism. When people are equipped with knowledge and critical thinking skills, they're ready to push for change in their communities, becoming drivers of cultural evolution. In today's digital world, activism can take many forms, from social media campaigns to grassroots initiatives, and the impact of informed participation is hard to overlook. The more individuals grasp the systems that contribute to stagnation, the better they can challenge those systems. Education, therefore, serves as a powerful tool for collective empowerment, guiding us to reimagine and reshape our cultural landscape.

To showcase the transformative power of education and media literacy, we can look at various voices in education and activism. Conversations with teachers, activists, and media experts reveal a rich array of experiences and insights. A teacher might share the excitement of seeing a student understand media bias for the first time, realizing they have the ability to question and challenge the narratives around them. An activist could recount experiences from community workshops where people analyze local news coverage, bringing attention to overlooked issues and building a network of informed advocates. These stories highlight a shared belief: education can spark real change.

Take, for instance, the media literacy organizations that have emerged to meet the urgent need for critical engagement in our hyper-connected world. They offer resources for educators, parents, and community leaders, creating spaces where discussions about media influence are common. These groups often encourage collaboration between schools and local communities, fostering intergenerational conversations that enhance our understanding of media literacy's importance. Such initiatives help individuals regain their agency in a media-saturated environment, resulting in a ripple effect that goes far beyond the classroom.

However, the road toward a more media-literate society isn't without hurdles. As we push for media literacy to be included in education, we also face ongoing challenges, such as funding shortages, a lack of trained educators, and institutional resistance that can slow progress, especially in underfunded communities. Yet, persistence matters. Grassroots movements that support media literacy often start small, igniting change from the bottom up. This kind of activism not only raises awareness but also tackles the inequalities in access to media education.

We also need to remember that learning doesn't stop when formal education ends. Lifelong learning is essential to keep up with the ever-changing media landscape. Adults must also seek out educational options that bolster their media literacy skills. This might mean attending a workshop on fact-checking, joining community discussions about media representation, or simply keeping up with new technologies. The pursuit of knowledge should never end. By doing so, we cultivate a culture of curiosity and engagement that crosses generational divides.

While the journey toward improved media literacy has its challenges, the potential for cultural renewal is enormous. By nurturing a society where individuals have the skills to engage critically with media, we set the stage for a more vibrant cultural environment. Informed consumers are more likely to support creativity, innovation, and diversity—elements that celebrate the richness of human experience rather than getting stuck in the monotony of recycled stories. As we collectively work to break free from cultural stagnation, the need for education and media literacy stands out as a powerful beacon of hope.

So, what does the future of our cultural landscape look like? It's a place where people no longer passively consume media but actively interact with it, questioning its origins, messages, and implications. It's a future where young people are educated not just in academics but also in the art of discernment, learning to navigate the complexities of media with confidence and insight. Imagine classrooms buzzing with discussions about representation in film, bias in journalism, and the ethical responsibilities of digital content creation. This is the fertile ground from which creativity and innovation can flourish.

In this new cultural environment, individuals won't just be spectators; they will be active participants in an ongoing conversation about culture, media, and society. They will celebrate a range of voices, challenge outdated narratives, and push for a more inclusive variety of expressions. The transformation won't occur overnight, but every small step toward media literacy helps build a collective momentum that can ultimately redefine our cultural experiences.

As we continue on this journey, let's keep in mind the tremendous impact of education and media literacy. Investing in the next generation is crucial for breaking free from the chains of cultural stagnation. By nurturing critical thinking, encouraging diverse viewpoints, and empowering individuals to thoughtfully engage with media, we set the stage for a cultural renaissance that values creativity and innovation. The possibilities are endless; all it takes is our commitment to educate, engage, and enlighten those around us. Together, we can create an era where media literacy becomes not just an essential skill but a core part of a rich and vibrant cultural landscape, seamlessly woven into the fabric of our society.

Vision for the Future

Imagine a world where creativity knows no limits—a place where ideas bounce off one another, igniting new innovations at every corner. In this world, people from all backgrounds come together, mixing their perspectives to create a cultural scene filled with diversity and endless possibilities. This vision isn't just a distant fantasy; it can become a real part of our lives through teamwork, embracing technology, re-engaging with our communities, and nurturing a sense of wonder. By actively working toward these goals, we can build an environment that honors artistic expression, uplifts different voices, and sparks a creative renaissance.

At the center of this cultural shift is collaborative creation, a powerful force that goes beyond individual talent. When people from different backgrounds, skills, and cultures join forces, amazing projects can unfold. Collaborative efforts aren't merely about combining different art forms; they're about creating a shared experience that makes a significant impact. Take, for instance, the work done by organizations like the Public Art Fund, which connects artists and communities to develop public art projects. These projects encourage conversations, challenge what we think, and help people feel a sense of belonging. Think about the murals that brighten our neighborhoods, the installations that revitalize urban spaces, and the performances that turn sidewalks into stages. These collaborations are more than just pretty pictures; they're transformative experiences that draw communities closer together, allowing people to find common ground through shared creativity.

This teamwork spirit is also evident in how different art forms blend together, blurring old boundaries and creating new ways to express ourselves. The growth of interdisciplinary projects—like those combining visual art with technology, dance with theater, or music with interactive experiences—fuels a fresh wave of creativity. A great example is teamLab, a Tokyo-based art collective that uses projection mapping and digital tech to create stunning, interactive environments that invite participation. Such initiatives not only challenge our views on art but also provide a platform for community involvement, enabling people from diverse backgrounds to share their own stories and experiences.

Collaborative creation also promotes inclusivity, making sure that various perspectives are heard and valued in our cultural narrative. Picture a theater production that includes performers from different language backgrounds or a music festival that highlights artists from underrepresented communities. These collaborations are vital for breaking down walls and enhancing the cultural fabric by celebrating the uniqueness of every individual. By bringing diverse voices into the creative process, we honor the richness of human experience and create art that resonates deeply with a wider audience.

As we think about a vibrant cultural future, we can't overlook the role of technology in driving positive change. In a time when digital platforms play such a big part in our lives, using technology to make the arts more creative and accessible is crucial. Imagine a world where artists can easily connect with audiences across the globe, where new talent can showcase their work without facing traditional barriers. Social media, streaming services, and virtual galleries are transforming how we experience art, breaking down geographic boundaries and making creativity available to everyone.

Think about the power of platforms like Instagram, which have become essential for artists to share their work and connect with audiences in real-time. Artists don't have to wait for gallery representation or traditional methods to validate their creativity anymore. They can build a following, share ideas, and collaborate with others with just a click. This shift has given rise to a new generation of resourceful and innovative artists who embrace their true selves.

Additionally, emerging technologies like virtual reality (VR) and augmented reality (AR) open up exciting new paths for artistic expression. Picture stepping into a virtual gallery where you can interact with art pieces, explore immersive installations, or even join live performances, no matter where you are. In this digital age, art isn't just found in museums; it's an ever-expanding universe of creativity accessible to anyone with an internet connection. However, with these advancements comes the need to use technology responsibly— making sure it amplifies voices rather than silencing them and that it promotes inclusivity rather than exclusivity.

Community engagement is another vital piece of a thriving cultural landscape. As we look ahead, it's essential to rekindle that sense of belonging that unites people around shared artistic efforts. This can take many forms, from local grassroots initiatives to large-scale festivals celebrating homegrown talent. When communities rally around the arts, they create spaces that nurture creativity, encourage collaboration, and foster a sense of pride in their cultural expressions.

Imagine a neighborhood festival where local artists, musicians, and performers unite to showcase their talents, turning streets into vibrant stages and galleries. These events not only celebrate local culture but also create opportunities for individuals to connect, share ideas, and discover new artistic expressions. Through community-driven efforts, we can breathe new life into local cultures, ensuring that artistic voices of all kinds are recognized and celebrated.

Moreover, community engagement encourages mentorship and skill-sharing, allowing experienced artists to guide emerging talents and help cultivate the next wave of creators. By building spaces where people can collaborate, share resources, and support one another, we empower communities to thrive through the arts. This sense of togetherness enriches the cultural landscape and creates a ripple effect, encouraging people to take pride in their creative contributions and support one another's efforts.

In imagining our future, nurturing a culture of curiosity is key to unlocking innovation and artistic evolution. When we inspire individuals to explore new ideas, experiment with different forms, and take risks in their artistic journeys, we create an atmosphere ripe for cultural growth. Curiosity fuels creativity, and when individuals feel empowered to ask questions, challenge norms, and venture into the unknown, they open the door to new possibilities.

Picture schools and community centers that prioritize curiosity-driven learning, cultivating an environment where students are encouraged to experiment with various forms of expression and think creatively. This might involve hosting workshops where participants explore unconventional materials, engage in interdisciplinary projects, or collaborate with local artists to bring their visions to life. By fostering a culture that values curiosity, we create a generation of thinkers, creators, and innovators who are fearless in pushing boundaries and redefining what's possible.

Plus, encouraging curiosity isn't limited to formal education. Art and culture should be part of our everyday lives, inspiring individuals to seek out new experiences, engage with a variety of expressions, and maintain an openness to learning. Imagine a community where art is not confined to galleries and stages but is woven into daily life, sparking spontaneous creativity everywhere. Street art, public installations, and interactive performances could become essential parts of the urban landscape, inspiring curiosity and encouraging exploration.

As we envision a future brimming with creativity, it's crucial to remember that each of us plays a part in shaping our cultural landscape. Engaging with these ideas allows us to become active participants in the world of art and culture. By embracing collaboration, leveraging technology, supporting community initiatives, and nurturing curiosity, we can help build a vibrant, dynamic society that celebrates creativity and innovation.

In this bright future, stagnation in culture will be a thing of the past. The barriers that once limited artistic expression will fall away, replaced by a landscape where ideas flow freely and creativity thrives. People will no longer just consume culture passively; they will become co-creators, actively involved in shaping the stories and expressions that define their communities. The potential for a cultural renaissance is limitless when we unite to champion creativity, celebrate differences, and cultivate an environment where innovation is welcomed and celebrated.

As we stand at this turning point, let's remember that the power to shape the future is in our hands. By reclaiming our agency and embracing collaboration, technology, community engagement, and curiosity, we can collectively create a cultural landscape that enriches our lives and inspires future generations. The road ahead may come with challenges, but the rewards will be immense. Together, we can create a world where creativity knows no bounds, where every voice is valued, and where a vibrant cultural landscape invites exploration, expression, and joy.

The future of culture is not just a dream we hold; it's something we actively create. It's a call for each of us to step up, engage with our communities, and contribute to the rich world of artistic expression that reflects our shared humanity. The possibilities are endless, and the time for action is now. Let's embrace the vision of a thriving cultural landscape, driven by creativity, collaboration, and inclusivity, and work together to turn this vision into a lively reality.

Conclusion

And there you have it, folks—a whirlwind tour through the endless rerun we call modern culture. We've dissected the corporate-sponsored nostalgia machine, peeked behind the curtain of algorithmic creativity, and stared into the abyss of our own comfort-seeking behavior. If you're feeling a bit dizzy, don't worry—that's just the vertigo from realizing we've been running in circles for the past two decades.

But fear not! Armed with the insights from this journey, you're now equipped to be a cultural revolutionary. Or at the very least, someone who can spot a reheated trend from a mile away. Remember, every time you choose to engage with something truly original, you're throwing a wrench into the gears of the great stagnation machine.

As we close this book and step back into the wild world of regurgitated content and "vintage" everything, ask yourself: Will you be a passive consumer in this time loop, or will you be the glitch that breaks the system? The choice is yours. You could start small—maybe try listening to a new genre of music that doesn't sound like it was made by a bot trained on your parents' record collection. Or go big—create that weird, wonderful thing that's been lurking in the back of your mind, even if it doesn't fit neatly into an Instagram aesthetic.

The future of culture is in our hands. It's time to shake off the comfortable blanket of familiarity and embrace the exhilarating uncertainty of true innovation. Who knows? The next big cultural revolution might start with you. Just don't let it turn into a franchise with diminishing returns and endless sequels.

Now go forth and create something that makes the algorithms scratch their virtual heads in confusion. The world is waiting for your fresh perspective—even if it doesn't know it yet.